THE 7 CONTINENTS

EUROPE

WITHDRAWN

D1290970

CONTENTS

Downloadable Maps

Nine maps used in this book are available for download on our Web site, as well as two color maps: one projection map of the world and one political map of Europe.

How to Download:

1. Go to www.evan-moor.com/resources.

2. Enter your e-mail address and the resource code for this product—EMC3735.

3. You will receive an e-mail with a link to the downloadable maps.

What's in This Book

▶ **5 sections** of reproducible information and activity pages centered on five main topics: Europe in the World, Political Divisions, Physical Features, Valuable Resources, and Culture.

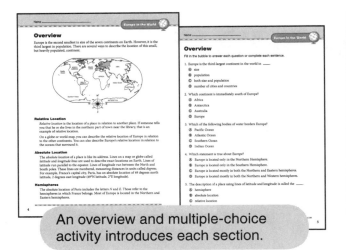

An overview and multiple-choice activity introduces each section.

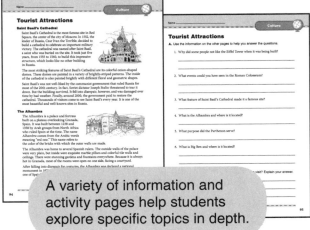

A variety of information and activity pages help students explore specific topics in depth.

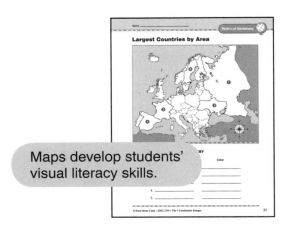

Maps develop students' visual literacy skills.

A crossword puzzle at the end of each section provides a fun review activity.

▶ **1 section** of assessment activities

▶ **1 section** of open-ended note takers

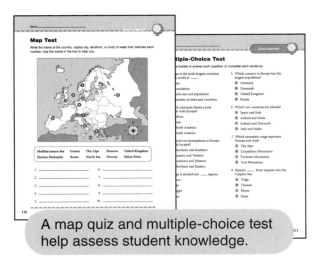

A map quiz and multiple-choice test help assess student knowledge.

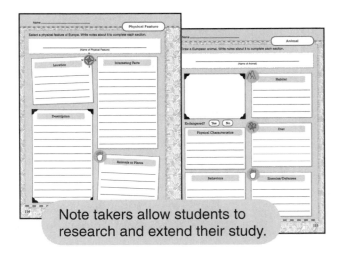

Note takers allow students to research and extend their study.

Europe in the World

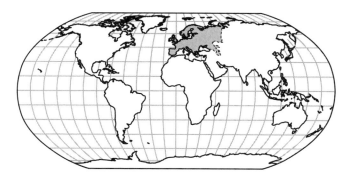

This section introduces students to the location of Europe in the world. Students learn about the difference between relative and absolute location, as well as the hemispheres in which Europe lies. Students also practice using lines of latitude and longitude to find places on a map.

Each skill in this section is based on the following National Geography Standards:

Essential Element 1: The World in Spatial Terms

Standard 1: How to use maps and other geographic representations, tools, and technologies to acquire, process, and report information from a spatial perspective

CONTENTS

Overview

Europe is the second smallest in size of the seven continents on Earth. However, it is the third largest in population. There are several ways to describe the location of this small, but heavily populated, continent.

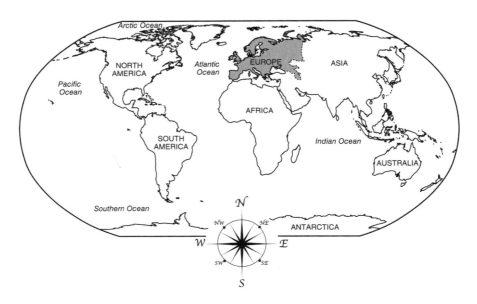

Relative Location

Relative location is the location of a place in relation to another place. If someone tells you that he or she lives in the northern part of town near the library, that is an example of relative location.

On a globe or world map, you can describe the relative location of Europe in relation to the other continents. You can also describe Europe's relative location in relation to the oceans that surround it.

Absolute Location

The *absolute location* of a place is like its address. Lines on a map or globe called *latitude* and *longitude lines* are used to describe exact locations on Earth. Lines of latitude run parallel to the equator. Lines of longitude run between the North and South poles. These lines are numbered, measuring distances in units called *degrees*. For example, France's capital city, Paris, has an absolute location of 49 degrees north latitude, 2 degrees east longitude (49°N latitude, 2°E longitude).

Hemispheres

The absolute location of Paris includes the letters *N* and *E*. Those refer to the hemispheres in which France belongs. Most of Europe is located in the Northern and Eastern hemispheres.

Overview

Fill in the bubble to answer each question or complete each sentence.

1. Europe is the third-largest continent in the world in _____.

   Ⓐ size

   Ⓑ population

   Ⓒ both size and population

   Ⓓ number of cities and countries

2. Which continent is immediately south of Europe?

   Ⓐ Africa

   Ⓑ Antarctica

   Ⓒ Australia

   Ⓓ Europe

3. Which of the following bodies of water borders Europe?

   Ⓐ Pacific Ocean

   Ⓑ Atlantic Ocean

   Ⓒ Southern Ocean

   Ⓓ Indian Ocean

4. Which statement is true about Europe?

   Ⓐ Europe is located only in the Northern Hemisphere.

   Ⓑ Europe is located only in the Southern Hemisphere.

   Ⓒ Europe is located mostly in both the Northern and Eastern hemispheres.

   Ⓓ Europe is located mostly in both the Northern and Western hemispheres.

5. The description of a place using lines of latitude and longitude is called the _____.

   Ⓐ hemisphere

   Ⓑ absolute location

   Ⓒ relative location

   Ⓓ intermediate direction

Europe's Relative Location

Relative location is the position of a place in relation to another place. How would you describe where Europe is located in the world using relative location?

Look at the world map on the other page. One way to describe Europe's relative location is to name the other continents that border it. For example, Europe is west of Asia and north of Africa.

Another way to describe the relative location of Europe is to name the bodies of water that surround the continent. For example, Europe is east of the Atlantic Ocean, south of the Arctic Ocean, and north of the Mediterranean Sea.

A. Use the map on the other page to complete the paragraph about the relative location of Europe.

Europe is the second-smallest continent in the world. It is located

west of the continent of _____. Africa is to the

_____ of Europe, and _____

is to the west. To the north is the cold _____ Ocean.

The Mediterranean Sea is _____ of Europe. The

_____ Ocean borders the continent to the west.

B. Follow the directions to color the map on the other page.

1. Color the continent immediately south of Europe green.

2. Color the continent west of Europe yellow.

3. Use blue to circle the name of the ocean that is west of Europe.

4. Draw a panda on the continent east of Europe.

Name

Europe's Relative Location

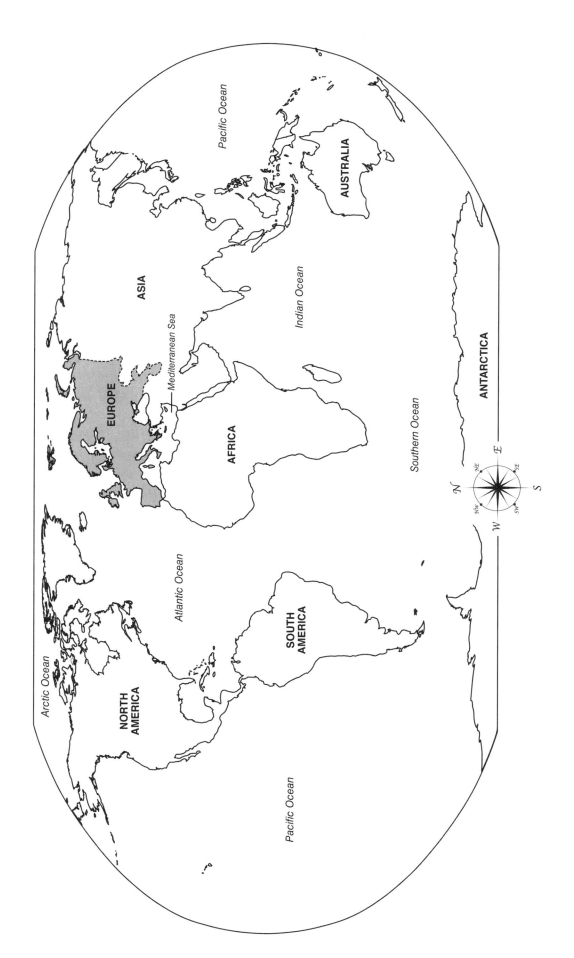

Arctic Ocean

NORTH
AMERICA

Pacific Ocean

Atlantic Ocean

SOUTH
AMERICA

ASIA

EUROPE

Mediterranean Sea

AFRICA

Pacific Ocean

Indian Ocean

AUSTRALIA

Southern Ocean

ANTARCTICA

Europe's Hemispheres

On a globe, Earth is divided into four hemispheres by a horizontal line called the *equator* and by vertical lines that run from the North Pole to the South Pole. The hemispheres are the Northern, Southern, Western, and Eastern. Europe is part of the Northern Hemisphere because it is north of the equator. Most of Europe is located in the Eastern Hemisphere, although a small part is in the Western Hemisphere as well.

Northern and Southern Hemispheres

A globe shows an imaginary horizontal line that runs around the center of Earth. This line is called the equator. The equator divides Earth into the Northern and Southern hemispheres.

Since all of Europe is north of the equator, the entire continent is in the Northern Hemisphere.

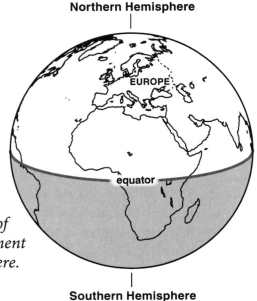

Western and Eastern Hemispheres

A globe also shows imaginary vertical lines that run from the North Pole to the South Pole. One of these vertical lines is called the *prime meridian*. This line, along with its twin line on the opposite side of the globe, create the Western and Eastern hemispheres.

Since most of Europe is east of the prime meridian, most of the continent is in the Eastern Hemisphere.

Name _____

Europe's Hemispheres

A. Write the letter of the definition that matches each term. Use the information on the other page to help you.

_____ 1. Europe

_____ 2. continent

_____ 3. globe

_____ 4. equator

_____ 5. Eastern Hemisphere

_____ 6. hemisphere

_____ 7. Western Hemisphere

_____ 8. Northern Hemisphere

_____ 9. prime meridian

a. an imaginary line that runs from the North Pole to the South Pole

b. half of Earth

c. the continent that is mostly in the Northern and Eastern hemispheres

d. the hemisphere that is east of the prime meridian

e. an imaginary line that divides Earth into the Northern and Southern hemispheres

f. one of the seven large landmasses of Earth

g. the hemisphere that is west of the prime meridian

h. a round model of Earth

i. the hemisphere that is north of the equator

B. Label the parts of the globe. Use the letters next to the terms in the box.

A. Eastern Hemisphere

B. Europe

C. Northern Hemisphere

D. equator

E. prime meridian

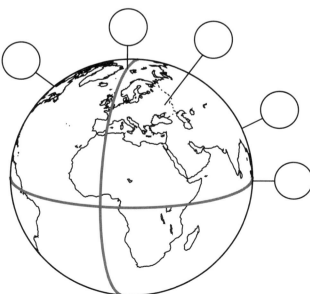

Europe's Absolute Location

Many globes contain lines that make it easier to find specific places on Earth. Lines of latitude measure the distance north and south of the equator. Lines of longitude measure the distance east and west of the prime meridian. You can use lines of latitude and longitude to find the absolute location of Europe on a globe.

Latitude

The equator is found at the absolute location of 0° (zero degrees) latitude. Other lines of latitude run parallel to the equator and are labeled with an *N* or *S*, depending on whether they are north or south of the equator. Latitude lines are also called *parallels*.

On the picture of the globe, notice the lines of latitude. Look for the continent of Europe. Since all of the continent is north of the equator, all of the latitude lines used to find the absolute location of places in Europe are labeled in *degrees north*, or °N.

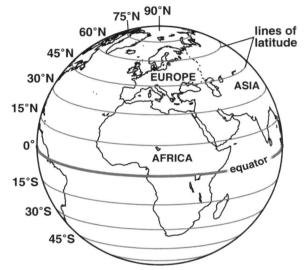

Lines of Latitude (Parallels)

Longitude

The prime meridian is an imaginary line that runs from the North Pole to the South Pole at 0° (zero degrees) longitude. Other lines of longitude run north and south, too, and are labeled with an *E* or *W*, depending on whether they are east or west of the prime meridian. Longitude lines are also called *meridians*.

On the picture of the globe, notice the lines of longitude. Look for the continent of Europe. Since most of the continent is east of the prime meridian, most of the longitude lines used to find the absolute location of places in Europe are labeled in *degrees east*, or °E. Some parts of Europe are west of the prime meridian. The absolute locations of those parts are labeled in *degrees west*, or °W.

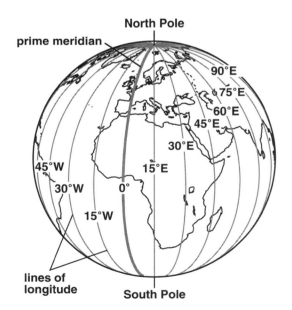

Lines of Longitude (Meridians)

Europe's Absolute Location

To find the absolute location of a place, read the latitude line first and then read the longitude line. For example, the latitude 40°N runs through the southern part of Italy. The longitude 15°E also runs through the southern part of Italy. So the absolute location of southern Italy is 40°N latitude, 15°E longitude.

A. Circle the correct answer to each question. Use the pictures of the globes and the information on the other page to help you.

1. Which line is at 0 degrees latitude?   **equator**   **prime meridian**

2. Which line runs north and south?   **equator**   **prime meridian**

3. In which direction is Europe from the equator?   **north**   **south**

4. Which line of longitude runs through Italy?   **15°W**   **15°E**

5. Where is the North Pole located?   **90°S**   **90°N**

6. Which lines run parallel to the equator?   **latitude lines**   **longitude lines**

7. How many degrees are between each line of latitude and longitude on the globe pictures?   **10 degrees**   **15 degrees**

8. What is another name for *lines of latitude*?   **meridians**   **parallels**

9. Which line of latitude runs through Europe?   **45°N**   **45°S**

10. What is another name for *lines of longitude*?   **parallels**   **meridians**

B. Using the information on this page and the other page, explain why southern Italy has an absolute location labeled in degrees north and east.

_____

_____

Using a Projection Map

How do you draw a picture of a round object, like Earth, on a flat piece of paper? In order to show all the continents and oceans in one view, mapmakers use a system called *projection*. Mapping the round Earth on a flat surface causes some areas to look bigger than they really are. For example, land near the poles gets stretched out when flattened. That's why Greenland and Antarctica look so big on some maps.

A projection map of the world shows all the lines of latitude and longitude on Earth. Study the projection map on the other page. Notice the lines of latitude and longitude. You can use these lines to find the absolute location of a specific place in Europe. For example, the label *Europe* is located at about 50°N latitude, 20°E longitude.

A. Read each statement. Circle **yes** if it is true or **no** if it is false. Use the map on the other page to help you.

1. The prime meridian runs through Europe.   **Yes**   **No**

2. Most of Europe is located between the longitudes of 0° and 30°E.   **Yes**   **No**

3. All of Europe is located between the latitudes of 45°N and 60°N.   **Yes**   **No**

4. Europe is the only continent east of the prime meridian.   **Yes**   **No**

5. Europe shares some of the same northern latitude lines with North America.   **Yes**   **No**

6. Europe shares some of the same eastern longitude lines with Australia.   **Yes**   **No**

7. The longitude line 15°E runs through Europe and Africa.   **Yes**   **No**

8. The latitude line 45°N runs through Europe and Asia.   **Yes**   **No**

9. There are no continents on 60°S latitude.   **Yes**   **No**

B. How many continents can you find on the map that share the longitude of 15°E? Write their names.

_____

Name _____

Using a Projection Map

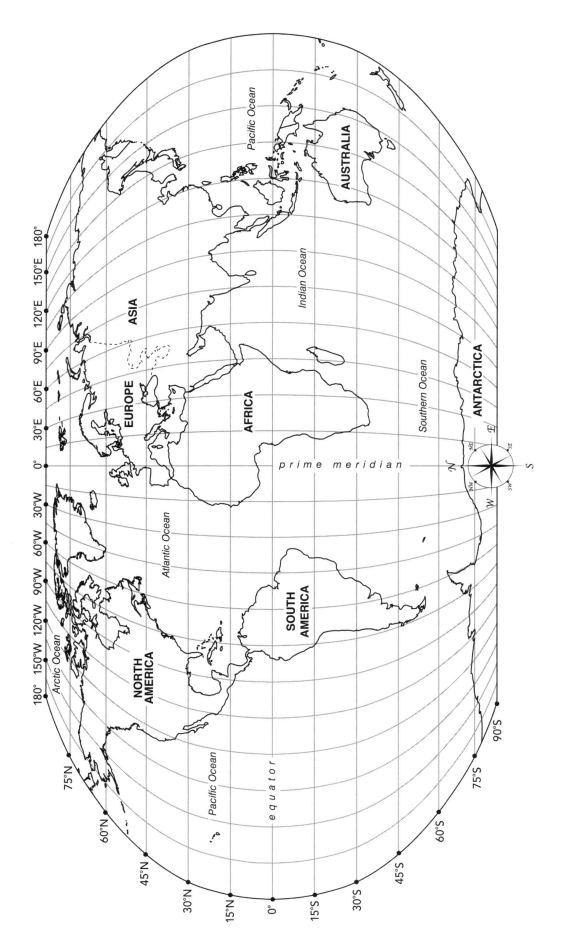

Review

Use words from the box to complete the crossword puzzle.

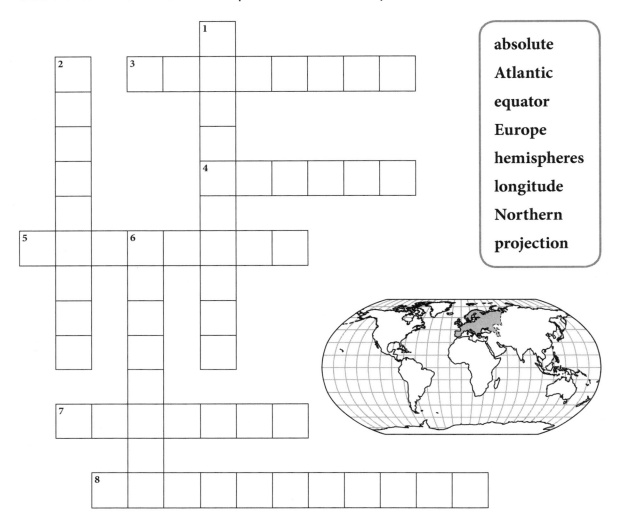

absolute
Atlantic
equator
Europe
hemispheres
longitude
Northern
projection

Across

3. All of Europe is located in the ____ Hemisphere.

4. ____ is west of Asia and north of Africa.

5. The ____ Ocean is west of Europe.

7. The ____ is an imaginary line that divides the Northern and Southern hemispheres.

8. The world is divided into four ____.

Down

1. A ____ map shows the round Earth on a flat surface.

2. Lines of ____ are also called meridians.

6. ____ location is used to find a specific place on Earth.

Political Divisions of Europe

This section introduces students to the four regions and 45 countries of Europe. Students study information about the largest countries in both area and population. They learn that the population of Europe varies significantly by region. Students also discover the changing nature of Europe's political divisions by reading about the former Soviet Union and the European Union.

Each skill in this section is based on the following National Geography Standards:

Essential Element 2: Places and Regions

Standard 5: That people create regions to interpret Earth's complexity

Essential Element 4: Human Systems

Standard 9: The characteristics, distribution, and migration of human populations on Earth's surface

CONTENTS

Overview

Europe is the sixth-largest continent in size and the third largest in population.

- Europe covers only about 7% of the world's landmass.

- Europe has about 11% of the world's population—729 million people.

The Four Regions

The 45 countries in Europe can be divided into four regions.

Region	Number of Countries	Fast Fact
Western Europe	9	includes the third-largest country in Europe (France)
Eastern Europe	10	is the largest and most populated region
Southern Europe	16	includes the smallest country in Europe (Holy See)
Northern Europe	10	is the least populated region

Where People Live

Although Europe is fairly small in size, the continent contains many people. This means that most of Europe is densely populated. The region with the highest population is Eastern Europe. About 263 million people live in this part of the continent. Western and Southern Europe are also highly populated, with 190 million and 145 million people, respectively.

Northern Europe, which includes 10 countries, has the smallest population of the four regions. Only about 97 million people live in this region. Iceland has the smallest population of the countries in Northern Europe. Fewer than 310,000 people live there.

Overview

Fill in the bubble to answer each question or complete each sentence.

1. Europe is the ____-largest continent in size.
   - Ⓐ fifth
   - Ⓑ fourth
   - Ⓒ sixth
   - Ⓓ second

2. There are ____ countries in Eastern Europe.
   - Ⓐ 9
   - Ⓑ 10
   - Ⓒ 16
   - Ⓓ 45

3. About 190 million people live in ____.
   - Ⓐ Northern Europe
   - Ⓑ Southern Europe
   - Ⓒ Western Europe
   - Ⓓ Eastern Europe

4. Which region contains the smallest country in Europe?
   - Ⓐ Southern Europe
   - Ⓑ Northern Europe
   - Ⓒ Eastern Europe
   - Ⓓ Western Europe

5. The Northern European country with the smallest population is ____.
   - Ⓐ Sweden
   - Ⓑ Iceland
   - Ⓒ Finland
   - Ⓓ Denmark

Population of Europe

A *population census* is a survey by a national government to gather information about the number of people who live in that country. Population censuses have been taken since ancient times. The earliest known population counts were made by the Chinese and Egyptians. Most countries today conduct an official census every 10 years. Experts look at the population figures from the past and present and try to predict what the population will be in the future.

Between 1950 and 2010, the world population nearly tripled to almost 7 billion. That number is expected to increase to 9 billion by 2050. The population of Europe is not growing as fast as the world's population. In 1950, there were about 547 million people living in Europe. The population grew to about 729 million in 2010. Experts estimate that the population will actually fall to about 650 million by 2050.

Europe's Population: 1950–2050

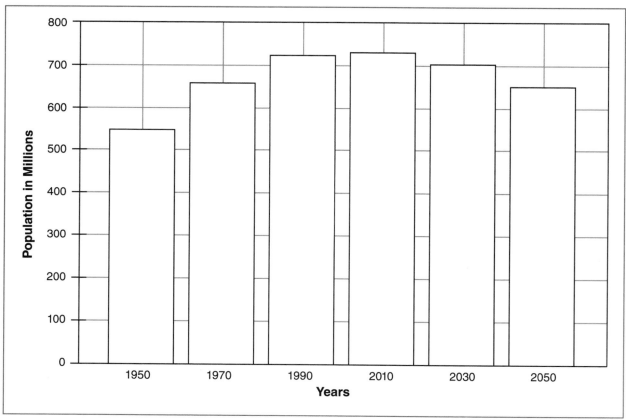

U.S. Bureau of the Census, International Data Base

A. Color each bar on the graph above a different color.

Population of Europe

B. Circle the correct answer. Use the information and graph on the other page to help you.

1. The population of the world has nearly _____ since 1950.

    doubled   **tripled**   **quadrupled**

2. It is predicted that there will be about 9 billion people in the world by _____.

    2030   **2050**   **2070**

3. Between 1970 and 2010, the population of Europe grew at a _____ rate.

    steady   **rapid**   **slow**

4. In 1950, there were about _____ million people living in Europe.

    657   **547**   **702**

5. In 2010, there were over _____ million people in Europe.

    500   **600**   **700**

6. By 2030, there will be about _____ million people in Europe.

    729   **650**   **702**

7. Between 2010 and 2050, the population of Europe is expected to _____.

    increase   **decline**   **stay the same**

8. The population increased the most between the years _____.

    1950–1970   **1970–1990**   **1990–2010**

C. Write two questions that can be answered using the information on the graph. Then answer the questions.

1. _____

    _____

2. _____

    _____

Countries of Europe

Europe is made up of 45 countries. The largest country in Europe is not actually a whole country, but a section of one—Russia. The rest of Russia is located in Asia. The smallest nation in Europe is the Holy See (Vatican City), which is located within the country of Italy. Europe also includes several island nations: the United Kingdom, which includes England, Northern Ireland, Scotland, and Wales; Ireland; Malta; and Iceland.

The chart below shows the four regions of Europe and the countries that are in each region.

Region	Countries	
Western	Austria Belgium France Germany Liechtenstein	Luxembourg Monaco Netherlands Switzerland
Eastern	Belarus Bulgaria Czech Republic Hungary Moldova	Poland Romania Russia Slovakia Ukraine
Southern	Albania Andorra Bosnia and Herzegovina Croatia Greece Holy See (Vatican City) Italy Kosovo	Macedonia Malta Montenegro Portugal San Marino Serbia Slovenia Spain
Northern	Denmark Estonia Finland Iceland Ireland	Latvia Lithuania Norway Sweden United Kingdom

regional designations determined by the United Nations

Look at the map on the other page. Use the information in the chart above to color the countries in each region of Europe according to the color key.

Color Key

Western Europe: Green   **Eastern Europe:** Orange
Southern Europe: Red   **Northern Europe:** Yellow

Countries of Europe

Bosnia & Herz. = Bosnia and Herzegovina

Czech Rep. = Czech Republic

Kos. = Kosovo

Liecht. = Liechtenstein

Lux. = Luxembourg

Mont. = Montenegro

Switz. = Switzerland

* A small part of Turkey is located in Europe, although most of the country is in Asia. The United Nations does not count Turkey as a European country.

Largest Countries by Area

Europe contains many countries that are fairly small in area. However, it also includes a part of Russia, the largest country in the world. Russia is so large that even though most of it is located in Asia, the "small" section that lies within Europe is still larger than any other European country. The next-largest country, Ukraine, is about one-sixth the size of the European part of Russia.

Largest Countries of Europe

	Country	Square Miles	Square Kilometers
1	European part of Russia	1,528,560	3,960,000
2	Ukraine	233,090	603,700
3	France	211,209	547,030
4	Spain	194,885	504,750
5	Sweden	173,732	449,964

A. Write three statements that can be made by using information in the chart.

1. _____

_____

2. _____

_____

3. _____

_____

B. On the map on the other page, you will see five numbered countries. The numbers indicate the rank of each country according to size. Color each country a different color. Then complete the map key by writing the country names in order from largest to smallest. Write the color you used on the map for each country.

Largest Countries by Area

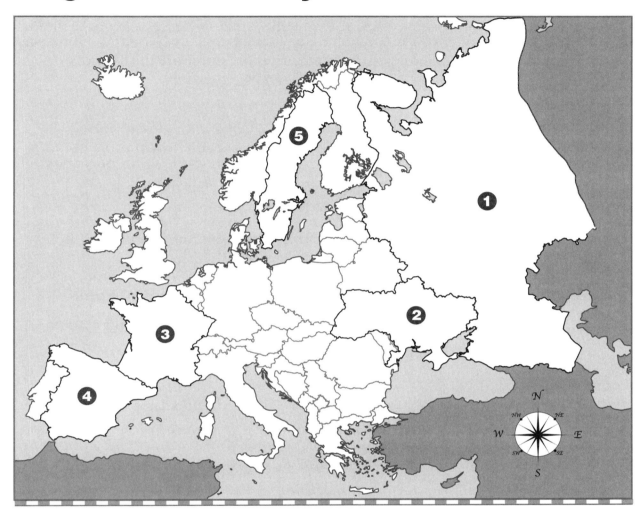

MAP KEY

The Five Largest Countries   **Color**

1. _____   _____

2. _____   _____

3. _____   _____

4. _____   _____

5. _____   _____

Largest Countries by Population

Europe contains many countries with high populations. The European part of Russia is the most populated country on the continent. Russia is followed by Germany and France. Completing the list of the 10 most populated countries in Europe are the United Kingdom, Italy, Ukraine, Spain, Poland, Romania, and Netherlands.

A. Next to the name of each country, write the letter of the clue that describes it. Use the information on this page and the chart on the other page to help you.

_____ 1. France

_____ 2. Germany

_____ 3. Italy

_____ 4. Poland

_____ 5. Romania

_____ 6. European Russia

_____ 7. Spain

_____ 8. Netherlands

_____ 9. Ukraine

_____ 10. United Kingdom

a. This part of a country has the largest population in Europe.

b. This country has fewer than 45 million people, but more than 40 million people.

c. This country has about 82 million people.

d. This country has about 3,000,000 more people than the United Kingdom.

e. This country has a population of 16,783,092.

f. This is the eighth most populated country.

g. This country has about 45.5 million people.

h. This country has about half the population of Ukraine.

i. This country has 61,284,806 people.

j. This country is ranked fifth in population.

B. Use the chart on the other page to help you answer these questions.

1. How many countries in Europe have populations over 60 million?   _____

2. How many of the 10 most populated countries in Europe have populations under 50 million?   _____

Largest Countries by Population

	Country	Population
1	European Russia	108,724,360
2	Germany	82,282,988
3	France	64,768,389
4	United Kingdom	61,284,806
5	Italy	58,090,681

	Country	Population
6	Ukraine	45,415,596
7	Spain	40,548,753
8	Poland	38,463,689
9	Romania	22,181,287
10	Netherlands	16,783,092

C. Use information from the chart above to write three statements about the most populated countries of Europe.

1. _____

_____

2. _____

_____

3. _____

_____

Western Europe

Western Europe contains nine countries and has a population of about 190 million. Some of the countries, such as Germany and France, are large in area and population. Others, such as Monaco and Liechtenstein, are so tiny that they are smaller than some U.S. cities!

With an area of nearly 248,429 square miles (643,428 square km), France is the largest country in Western Europe. It is slightly smaller than the state of Texas.

Germany has the highest population in Western Europe, with about 82 million people. Between 1949 and 1990, Germany was divided into two countries called West Germany and East Germany. In 1990, the two countries united into one nation.

A. Read each statement. Circle **yes** if it is true or **no** if it is false. Use the information on this page and the map on the other page to help you.

1.	There are 19 countries in Western Europe.	**Yes**	**No**
2.	Germany is the largest country in Western Europe.	**Yes**	**No**
3.	Monaco is a very small country.	**Yes**	**No**
4.	About 190 million people live in Western Europe.	**Yes**	**No**
5.	Liechtenstein is a large city in Western Europe.	**Yes**	**No**
6.	Ireland is not located in Western Europe.	**Yes**	**No**
7.	France is almost the size of Texas.	**Yes**	**No**
8.	Austria is a country in Western Europe.	**Yes**	**No**
9.	Luxembourg is wedged between Switzerland and Austria.	**Yes**	**No**
10.	Germany was divided into two countries for 41 years.	**Yes**	**No**

B. On the map on the other page, color each country a different color. Then write a caption about Western Europe under the map. Use the information on this page to help you.

Western Europe

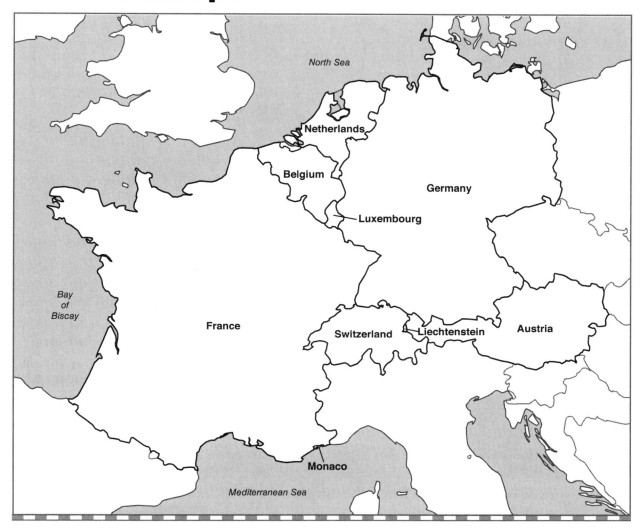

Eastern Europe

There are 10 countries in Eastern Europe. This area is a highly populated part of Europe, with about 263 million people. Four of the 10 most populated countries of the continent are located in Eastern Europe.

The European section of Russia is the most populated area within Eastern Europe, as well as the entire continent. Nearly 110 million people live in this part of Russia. Other Eastern European countries with large populations are Poland, Romania, Ukraine, and the Czech Republic.

There are many beautiful and world-famous capital cities in Eastern Europe. Some of these cities include Moscow, Russia; Prague, Czech Republic; and Budapest, Hungary.

A. Circle the correct answer to complete each sentence. Use the information on this page and the map on the other page to help you.

1. Eastern Europe has a population of about **220 million / 260 million**.

2. More than 110 million people live in the European part of **Romania / Russia**.

3. Poland, Romania, and Ukraine all have **small populations / large populations**.

4. Of the 10 most populated countries of Europe, **four / six** are in Eastern Europe.

5. Romania is larger in size than **Slovakia / Ukraine**.

6. Moscow is the capital of **Russia / Hungary**.

7. The capital city of the Czech Republic is **Budapest / Prague**.

8. The capital of **Hungary / Romania** is Budapest.

B. On the map on the other page, color the five most populated countries of Eastern Europe red. Then write the names of the capital cities of the Czech Republic, Hungary, and Russia next to the stars.

Eastern Europe

Barents Sea

Russia

Baltic Sea

Russia

Belarus

Poland

Czech
Republic

Slovakia

Ukraine

Moldova

Hungary

Romania

Bulgaria

Black Sea

Caspian Sea

Southern Europe

With 16 nations, Southern Europe has more countries than any other region of Europe. A small portion of Turkey is also located in this region, although it is not recognized by the United Nations as part of Europe.

Italy has the largest population of Southern Europe, with more than 58 million people. It is followed by Spain, which has 40 million people and is the largest country in size. However, most of Southern Europe's countries are small in both size and population. Andorra has about 84,000 people and its area is only two-and-a-half times bigger than Washington, D.C. And the country of the Holy See, the central government of the Catholic Church, is located within the city of Rome. It has only about 800 people!

Countries of Southern Europe

Country	Population	Area
Albania	3,659,616	11,100 square miles (28,748 square km)
Andorra	83,888	181 square miles (468 square km)
Bosnia & Herzegovina	4,621,598	19,758 square miles (51,187 square km)
Croatia	4,486,881	21,845 square miles (56,579 square km)
Greece	10,749,943	50,949 square miles (131,957 square km)
Holy See (Vatican City)	829	0.17 square mile (0.44 square km)
Italy	58,090,681	116,317 square miles (301,340 square km)
Kosovo	1,804,838	4,203 square miles (10,887 square km)
Macedonia	2,072,086	9,819 square miles (25,433 square km)
Malta	406,771	124 square miles (320 square km)
Montenegro	666,730	5,333 square miles (13,812 square km)
Portugal	10,735,765	35,547 square miles (92,090 square km)
San Marino	31,477	24 square miles (61 square km)
Serbia	7,344,847	29,905 square miles (77,474 square km)
Slovenia	2,003,136	7,825 square miles (20,273 square km)
Spain	40,548,753	195,073 square miles (505,370 square km)

A. On the map on the other page, find Southern Europe's five largest countries in size. Color each of them a different color and then complete the map key.

Southern Europe

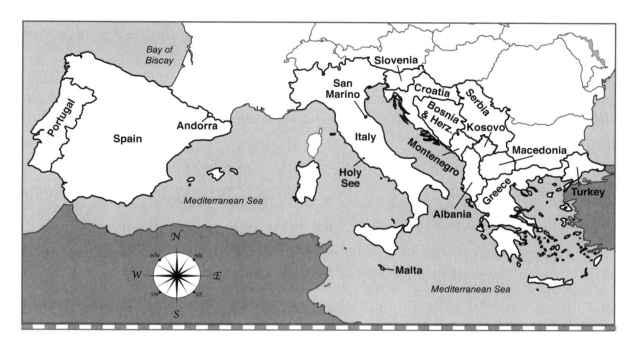

MAP KEY

The Five Largest Countries	Color
1. _____	_____
2. _____	_____
3. _____	_____
4. _____	_____
5. _____	_____

B. Write a caption for the map using the words *area*, *largest*, and *smallest*.

_____

_____

Northern Europe

Northern Europe is the least populated region in Europe, partly due to its fairly cold climate. There are 10 countries in Northern Europe. These countries are sometimes grouped into three regions: Scandinavia, the British Isles, and the Baltic states. Sweden, Norway, Denmark, and Finland are part of Scandinavia. The island nation of Iceland is sometimes considered Scandinavian as well. The United Kingdom and Ireland are part of the British Isles, and Estonia, Latvia, and Lithuania are considered the Baltic states.

Sweden is the largest country in Northern Europe, covering more than 173,000 square miles (449,964 square km). Finland is also large, at about 131,000 square miles (339,290 square km). But the United Kingdom, which includes England, Northern Ireland, Scotland, and Wales, has the largest population, with just over 61 million people. Iceland has the smallest population in Northern Europe, at about 309,000 people.

A. Read each statement. Circle **yes** if it is true or **no** if it is false. Use the information on this page and the map on the other page to help you.

1. There are nine nations in Northern Europe.   **Yes**   **No**

2. Wales is considered part of the British Isles.   **Yes**   **No**

3. Norway is part of Scandinavia.   **Yes**   **No**

4. Finland is the largest country in Northern Europe.   **Yes**   **No**

5. The Baltic states include Estonia, Latvia, and Lithuania.   **Yes**   **No**

6. Sweden has an area of more than 173,000 square miles.   **Yes**   **No**

7. Iceland is an island.   **Yes**   **No**

8. Iceland has the largest population in Northern Europe.   **Yes**   **No**

9. More than 61 million people live in the United Kingdom.   **Yes**   **No**

10. Northern Europe has a very large population.   **Yes**   **No**

B. Look at the map on the other page. Color each Northern European country using the color given for its region in the color key. Then write a caption to go with the map.

Northern Europe

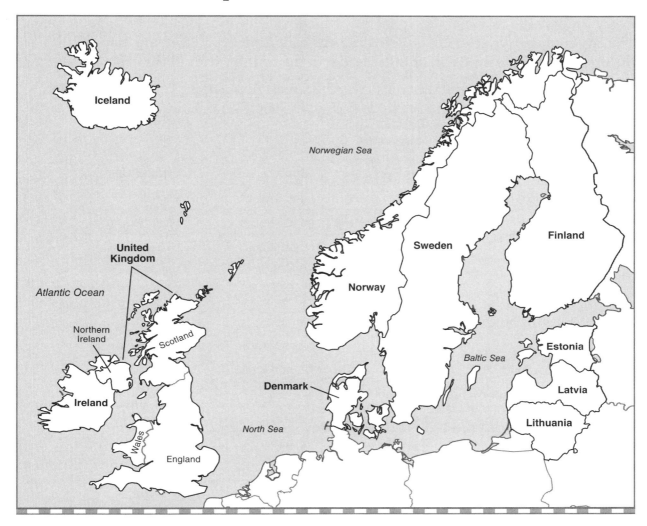

Color Key

Scandinavia: Orange   **British Isles:** Green   **Baltic states:** Red

_____

_____

Capital Cities of Europe

Every country in Europe has a capital city, which is the central location of its government. The city contains government buildings where leaders meet and laws are made. Often, the president, prime minister, or other leader of the country lives in the capital city.

In many countries, the capital city also has the largest population. For example, Moscow is both the capital and the largest city of Russia. In Switzerland, however, the capital is not the largest city.

Country	Capital City	Country	Capital City
Albania	Tirana	Lithuania	Vilnius
Andorra	Andorra la Vella	Luxembourg	Luxembourg
Austria	Vienna	Macedonia	Skopje
Belarus	Minsk	Malta	Valletta
Belgium	Brussels	Moldova	Chisinau
Bosnia & Herzegovina	Sarajevo	Monaco	Monaco
Bulgaria	Sofia	Montenegro	Podgorica
Croatia	Zagreb	Netherlands	Amsterdam
Czech Republic	Prague	Norway	Oslo
Denmark	Copenhagen	Poland	Warsaw
Estonia	Tallinn	Portugal	Lisbon
Finland	Helsinki	Romania	Bucharest
France	Paris	Russia	Moscow
Germany	Berlin	San Marino	San Marino
Greece	Athens	Serbia	Belgrade
Holy See	Vatican City	Slovakia	Bratislava
Hungary	Budapest	Slovenia	Ljubljana
Iceland	Reykjavik	Spain	Madrid
Ireland	Dublin	Sweden	Stockholm
Italy	Rome	Switzerland	Bern
Kosovo	Pristina	Ukraine	Kiev
Latvia	Riga	United Kingdom	London
Liechtenstein	Vaduz		

Capital Cities of Europe

A. Label the capital cities of France, Germany, Italy, Ukraine, and the United Kingdom.

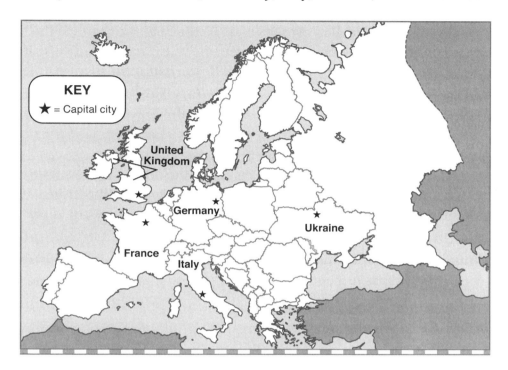

B. Write the letter of each country next to the correct capital city. Use the chart on the other page to help you.

_____ 1. Dublin	a. Austria
_____ 2. Bucharest	b. Czech Republic
_____ 3. Vienna	c. Denmark
_____ 4. Oslo	d. Ireland
_____ 5. Stockholm	e. Netherlands
_____ 6. Prague	f. Norway
_____ 7. Amsterdam	g. Poland
_____ 8. Kiev	h. Romania
_____ 9. Copenhagen	i. Sweden
_____ 10. Warsaw	j. Ukraine

Communism in Europe

At one time, many European countries were part of a huge nation called the USSR, more commonly known as the Soviet Union. The Soviet Union existed from 1917 until 1991 and had a type of government called *communism*. In the Soviet Union, all the land and means to produce goods were owned by the government. Residents had very little freedom, and life was hard for many people. In 1991, the communist government fell, and the Soviet Union was divided into a number of *republics*, which later became countries. The European countries of Belarus, Estonia, Latvia, Lithuania, Moldova, Russia, and Ukraine were all part of the Soviet Union.

There were several other countries in Europe that were not part of the Soviet Union but became communist after World War II in 1945. These included Albania, Bulgaria, Hungary, Poland, and Romania. Their communist governments fell between 1989 and 1991. The countries then became *democracies*, meaning that citizens could elect their leaders.

After the fall of communism, many former communist countries were divided into smaller countries. For example, Yugoslavia split into Bosnia and Herzegovina, Croatia, Kosovo, Macedonia, Montenegro, Serbia, and Slovenia. Czechoslovakia became the Czech Republic and Slovakia.

Complete the sentences using the information above and the map on the other page.

1. The USSR was a _____ country located in both Europe and Asia.

2. When communism fell in 1991, the Soviet Union split into several

   _____, which later became countries.

3. The Czech Republic and Slovakia once formed a country called

   _____.

4. A _____ is a type of government in which the people elect their own leaders.

5. The communist country of Yugoslavia split into _____ smaller countries.

Communism in Europe

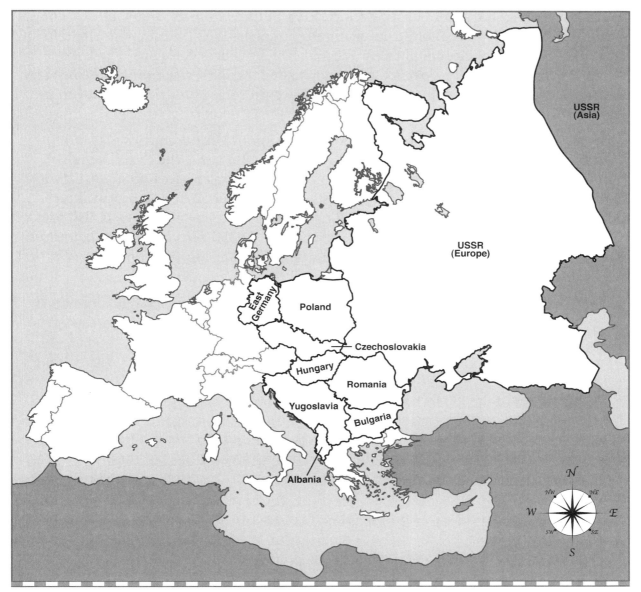

This map shows communist countries in Europe before the fall of communism.

European Union

In 1993, several countries in Europe decided to form the *European Union*, or EU. The idea was to establish an economic union among countries. Each country agreed to follow the same laws and policies about free trade and other business decisions. The European Union also created its own *currency*, or money, called the *Euro*, to eliminate the need for a different type of currency in every country. However, some countries continue to use their own currency.

Today, 27 countries are members of the European Union. More countries may join in the future. The current members are Austria, Belgium, Bulgaria, the Czech Republic, Denmark, Estonia, Finland, France, Germany, Greece, Hungary, Ireland, Italy, Latvia, Lithuania, Luxembourg, Malta, Netherlands, Poland, Portugal, Romania, Slovakia, Slovenia, Spain, Sweden, and the United Kingdom. The country of Cyprus is also part of the European Union, even though it is located in Asia. Citizens of all these countries do not need a passport to travel from one European Union country to another.

A. Read each statement. Circle **yes** if it is true or **no** if it is false. Use the information above to help you.

1. The European Union was formed in 1993.   **Yes**   **No**

2. Members of the EU follow the same policies on free trade.   **Yes**   **No**

3. Every country of the EU uses its own separate currency.   **Yes**   **No**

4. Russia is a country in the EU.   **Yes**   **No**

5. EU residents need a passport to travel to other EU countries. **Yes**   **No**

6. There are 27 members of the European Union.   **Yes**   **No**

7. No more countries can join the European Union.   **Yes**   **No**

8. Bulgaria is a member of the EU.   **Yes**   **No**

9. The United Kingdom is not an EU member.   **Yes**   **No**

10. Cyprus is a country in Europe.   **Yes**   **No**

B. Use green to color the countries of the European Union on the map on the other page.

European Union

Review

Use words from the box to complete the crossword puzzle.

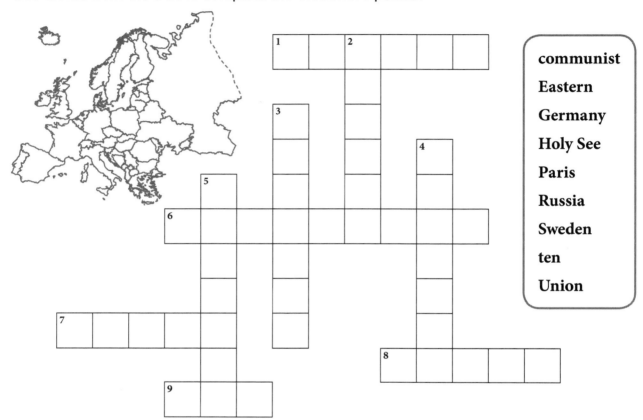

communist

Eastern

Germany

Holy See

Paris

Russia

Sweden

ten

Union

Across

1. This country is in both Europe and Asia.

6. Some European countries were once run by _____ governments.

7. _____ is the capital of France.

8. There are 27 countries in the European _____.

9. There are _____ countries in Northern Europe.

Down

2. This country is part of Scandinavia.

3. the most populated country of Western Europe

4. The most populated region in Europe is _____ Europe.

5. The _____ is a country with only 800 inhabitants.

Physical Features of Europe

This section introduces students to the landforms and bodies of water of Europe. Students discover that Europe has major mountain ranges, dense forests, frozen tundra, and vast plains, as well as peninsulas, volcanoes, and islands. Students also become familiar with Europe's major oceans, seas, rivers, and lakes.

Each skill in this section is based on the following National Geography Standards:

Essential Element 2:	Places and Regions
Standard 4:	The physical and human characteristics of places
Essential Element 3:	Physical Systems
Standards 7 & 8:	The physical processes that shape the patterns of Earth's surface, and the characteristics and spatial distribution of ecosystems on Earth's surface

CONTENTS

Overview

Although it is considered a separate continent, Europe shares the same landmass with Asia. No body of water separates the two completely. The main division between the two continents is the Ural Mountains. Europe is west of the Urals.

Even though Europe is a small continent, it has many different physical features, including some of the world's most famous landforms and bodies of water.

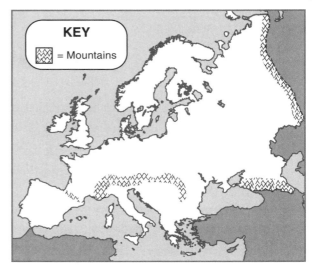

KEY

= Mountains

Landforms

Europe has five major mountain ranges. The Urals and the Caucasus Mountains separate Europe from Asia. The Alps stretch across parts of France, Italy, Switzerland, and Austria. The Pyrenees Mountains are located between France and Spain. And the Carpathian Mountains are situated in Eastern Europe.

Thick forests cover a good portion of Europe, especially in Germany and Russia. Flat plains and plateaus are found in Northern Europe, while frozen *tundra* blankets the northern parts of Scandinavia as well as Iceland.

Much of Europe is a collection of *peninsulas*, or land surrounded by water on three sides. The Scandinavian and Jutland peninsulas are located in Northern Europe. In Southern Europe, three peninsulas—the Iberian, Italian, and Balkan—extend into the Mediterranean Sea.

Europe also has many islands. The United Kingdom, Ireland, Iceland, and Malta are island nations. Numerous smaller islands, such as Sicily, Sardinia, Guernsey, Jersey, Corsica, and Crete, are territories belonging to other countries.

Bodies of Water

The Atlantic Ocean borders Europe to the west, while the Arctic Ocean is to the north. Europe is also bordered by several large seas, including the Mediterranean, Black, Norwegian, and North seas.

Europe has several major rivers, including the Rhine River in Germany, the Thames River in England, the Danube River in Eastern Europe, the Seine River in France, and the Volga River in Russia.

Overview

Fill in the bubble to answer each question or complete each sentence.

1. Which mountain range forms the main division between Europe and Asia?
   Ⓐ Ural Mountains
   Ⓑ Carpathian Mountains
   Ⓒ The Alps
   Ⓓ Pyrenees Mountains

2. France and Spain are separated by which mountain range?
   Ⓐ Pyrenees Mountains
   Ⓑ Carpathian Mountains
   Ⓒ The Alps
   Ⓓ Ural Mountains

3. Flat plains are found mostly in ＿＿ Europe.
   Ⓐ Eastern
   Ⓑ Western
   Ⓒ Southern
   Ⓓ Northern

4. Which two peninsulas are located in Northern Europe?
   Ⓐ Scandinavian and Iberian
   Ⓑ Iberian and Balkan
   Ⓒ Scandinavian and Jutland
   Ⓓ Jutland and Italian

5. The ＿＿ is a major river in England.
   Ⓐ Seine
   Ⓑ Thames
   Ⓒ Rhine
   Ⓓ Danube

Europe's Diverse Landscape

Europe's landscape is as diverse as its people. To the north, frozen tundra covers parts of Iceland and Scandinavia. But Southern Europe features warm coastal areas and tall mountain ranges. Plains are found in Northern Europe, as well as areas of Western and Eastern Europe. And forests cover nearly half of the continent.

Even though it is one of the smallest continents, Europe has a longer coastline than Africa, the second-largest continent. This is because Europe's coastline has an extremely jagged shape and includes several large peninsulas that jut away from the main landmass. Europe also has many islands, including the countries of Iceland, Ireland, and the United Kingdom.

A. Use the map on the other page to answer the questions.

1. Which mountain range is located above the Italian Peninsula? _____

2. What is the name of the major peak shown on the map? _____

3. Which islands are west of the North Sea? _____

4. Which mountain range is northeast of the Central Russian Upland? _____

5. What is the name of the plain that is south of the Baltic Sea? _____

6. Which peninsula is farthest west? _____

7. Which peninsula is shaped like a boot? _____

8. What is the name of the peninsula that is north of the Baltic Sea? _____

B. Write two facts about Europe's landscape. Use the information above and the map on the other page to help you.

1. _____

2. _____

Europe's Diverse Landscape

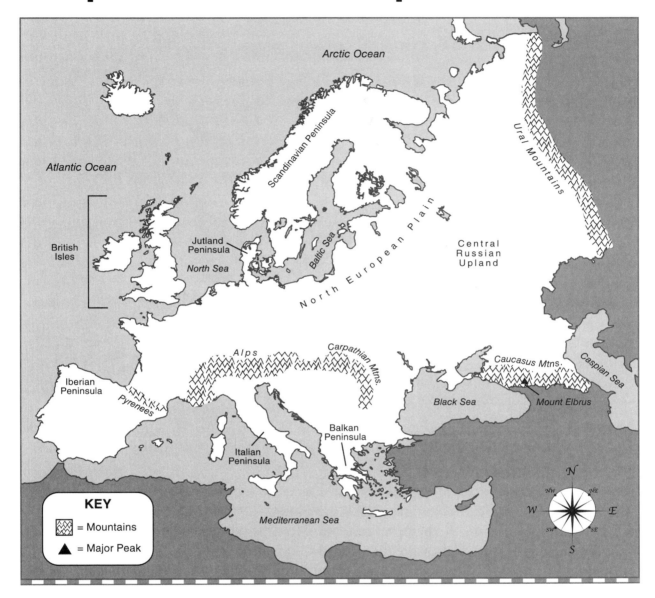

European Peninsulas

A peninsula is an area of land that is surrounded by water on three sides. Europe is a continent with many peninsulas. In fact, the continent itself could be considered one big peninsula of Asia. Europe's major peninsulas are the large Scandinavian, Balkan, and Iberian peninsulas, as well as the smaller Italian and Jutland peninsulas.

The Scandinavian Peninsula includes the countries of Norway and Sweden. A small portion of Finland is also located on the peninsula. Surrounded by the Baltic Sea, North Sea, and Norwegian Sea, the Scandinavian Peninsula is about 1,150 miles (1,850 km) long. Twenty-five percent of its land is located north of the Arctic Circle, where the climate is very cold.

Also in the north, the Jutland Peninsula contains Denmark and a small part of Germany. The peninsula extends into the North Sea and Baltic Sea. Flat plains and low hills make up most of this region.

The Balkan Peninsula, also called the Balkans, is located in southeastern Europe. It is surrounded by the Adriatic, Ionian, and Aegean seas. Albania, Bosnia and Herzegovina, Bulgaria, Croatia, Greece, Kosovo, Macedonia, Montenegro, part of Romania, Serbia, Slovenia, and European Turkey are all on the Balkan Peninsula. The region is very mountainous and contains several densely forested areas. The southernmost and coastal lands of the peninsula have a mild Mediterranean climate.

The Iberian Peninsula is located on the southwestern tip of Europe and includes the countries of Spain, Portugal, and Andorra. The Bay of Biscay, Atlantic Ocean, and Mediterranean Sea surround this peninsula, which is only 5 miles (8 km) away from Africa at its nearest point.

The boot-shaped Italian peninsula is located in Southern Europe and forms the country of Italy. The tiny countries of the Holy See (Vatican City) and San Marino are also located on the Italian Peninsula, which extends more than 600 miles (965 km) into the Mediterranean, Adriatic, and Ionian seas and is only 150 miles (240 km) across at its widest point.

European Peninsulas

A. Read each statement. Circle **yes** if it is true or **no** if it is false. Use the information on the other page to help you.

1. There are five major peninsulas in Europe.   **Yes**   **No**

2. The Scandinavian Peninsula includes part of Finland.   **Yes**   **No**

3. The Balkan Peninsula is located in Northern Europe.   **Yes**   **No**

4. Norway and Sweden are on the Jutland Peninsula.   **Yes**   **No**

5. The Baltic Sea borders the Iberian Peninsula.   **Yes**   **No**

6. The Italian Peninsula includes the country of the Holy See.   **Yes**   **No**

7. Spain and Portugal are on the same peninsula.   **Yes**   **No**

8. The Balkan Peninsula is shaped like a boot.   **Yes**   **No**

9. The continent of Europe itself could be considered a peninsula.   **Yes**   **No**

10. The Scandinavian Peninsula is close to Africa.   **Yes**   **No**

B. Write the name of the peninsula—*Scandinavian, Balkan, Iberian, Italian,* or *Jutland*—that answers each question.

1. Which peninsula is partly located above the Arctic Circle?   _____

2. Which peninsula is farthest west in Europe?   _____

3. Which peninsula contains 12 countries?   _____

4. Which peninsula is surrounded by the Baltic, North, and Norwegian seas?   _____

5. Which peninsula is 150 miles across at its widest point?   _____

6. Which peninsula includes the country of Denmark?   _____

European Islands

Many islands lie off the coasts of Europe. Some islands are independent countries, while others are territories belonging to European nations. A number of larger islands are located in the northern part of the continent. Thousands of smaller islands dot the Mediterranean and Aegean seas.

The British Isles

Northwest of the European mainland are the British Isles. The British Isles consist of two main islands—the United Kingdom and Ireland—as well as thousands of smaller islands. These smaller islands include the Isle of Man, Guernsey, and Jersey, which are three territories of the UK. Mountain ranges, plateaus, and valleys make up most of the northern and western United Kingdom. To the south, there are low hills and plains. Ireland, often called the Emerald Isle, is an island known for its lush green land and cool, rainy weather.

Faroe Islands

The Faroe Islands are an *archipelago,* or a group of islands, due north of the UK. They are surrounded by the North Atlantic Ocean and Norwegian Sea. Denmark governs the Faroe Islands, which are about eight times the size of Washington, D.C., when put together. The islands are rugged and rocky and feature high cliffs along the coasts.

Iceland

Northwest of the Faroe Islands, in the North Atlantic Ocean, is the island nation of Iceland. Iceland is actually the top of an underwater volcano. The island formed when a volcano under the ocean erupted and sent hot lava to the surface. When the lava cooled, it turned into rock, and a landmass was formed. Iceland is known for its many volcanoes, hot springs, and geysers. Because the island is situated far north, it also has several glaciers. Grassy lowlands, however, stretch along its coast.

Islands of the South

There are thousands of islands in the Mediterranean and Aegean seas in Southern Europe. The islands of Sicily and Sardinia are the biggest and belong to Italy. Sardinia lies west of the Italian Peninsula, while Sicily is the piece of land that looks like it's being "kicked" by Italy's boot. South of Sicily is Malta, which is an independent country composed of five islands. At the northeastern tip of Sardinia is the French island of Corsica. This mountainous island has more than 45 peaks over 6,560 feet (2,000 m) high.

In the Aegean Sea, there are more than 2,000 islands that belong to Greece. The largest Greek island is Crete. This island includes a high mountain range, plateaus, gorges, and caves. There are also many valleys and small plains along the coast.

European Islands

A. Circle the islands or island groups on the map using the colors given below.

Iceland

Faroe Islands

Ireland

United Kingdom

Isle of Man

Guernsey

Jersey

Corsica

Sardinia

Sicily

Malta

Greek Isles

Crete

Color Key

British Isles: green

Crete, Greek Isles: yellow

Corsica: purple

Faroe Islands: orange

Iceland: blue

Malta: brown

Sardinia, Sicily: red

B. Find and circle the names of the European islands.
Words may appear across, down, or diagonally.

```
U  Q  N  E  T  U  Y  C  R  E  T  E  M  F  V
S  C  J  S  A  L  T  I  C  E  L  A  N  D  K
A  B  L  C  N  R  M  Q  U  D  K  B  M  E  L
R  V  F  O  R  T  I  A  N  L  A  R  B  L  A
D  I  I  R  G  R  A  C  L  S  L  E  J  A  I
I  R  S  S  S  K  I  C  H  T  S  P  O  B  R
N  N  L  I  W  I  J  T  Y  K  A  H  L  E  E
I  J  A  C  M  A  C  F  A  R  O  E  R  N  L
A  I  F  A  R  Y  L  I  F  L  W  T  B  L  A
G  R  M  Y  W  U  F  D  L  J  R  Q  D  A  N
D  D  G  U  E  R  N  S  E  Y  E  U  M  D  D
O  U  N  I  T  E  D  K  I  N  G  D  O  M  P
```

Corsica

Crete

Faroe

Iceland

Ireland

Guernsey

Malta

Sicily

Sardinia

United Kingdom

Mountains of Europe

Europe has five major mountain ranges. Two ranges divide Europe from Asia. The Ural Mountains form the eastern border of Europe through Russia. And the Caucasus Mountains are located along the border between southeastern Russia and the Asian countries of Azerbaijan and Georgia. The highest mountain in Europe, Mount Elbrus, is in the Caucasus range. It stands 18,510 feet (5,642 meters) high.

The Alps run through France, Italy, Switzerland, and Austria. The high, snow-capped peaks of the Alps are known throughout the world for their beauty. Mont Blanc is the tallest mountain in the Alps, standing 15,781 feet (4,810 meters) high. This area of the Alps also includes deep valleys and lakes that were formed by glaciers. Three of Europe's largest rivers—the Rhine, the Rhone, and the Po—start in the Alps.

The Carpathian Mountains are located in the Czech Republic, Hungary, Poland, Romania, Slovakia, and Ukraine. Valleys divide the area into smaller mountain ranges. Gerlachovsky Peak, in Slovakia, is the highest Carpathian mountain.

The Pyrenees Mountains stretch between France and Spain and separate the Iberian Peninsula from the rest of the continent. This mountain chain is about 270 miles (430 km) long and 80 miles (130 km) wide.

Europe has several other smaller mountain ranges, including the Sierra Nevada range in southern Spain, the Rila range in Bulgaria, and the Jotunheimen Mountains in Norway. There are also a few mountains and volcanoes that are not part of a range. For example, Mount Etna in Sicily is a stand-alone volcano.

Some of Europe's Highest Mountains

Mountain	Height	Range	Location
Mount Elbrus	18,510 feet (5,642 m)	Caucasus	Russia
Dykh-Tau	17,077 feet (5,205 m)	Caucasus	Russia
Koshtan-Tau	16,896 feet (5,150 m)	Caucasus	Russia
Mont Blanc	15,781 feet (4,810 m)	Alps	Italy/France
Monte Rosa	15,200 feet (4,634 m)	Alps	Italy/Switzerland
The Dom	14,911 feet (4,545 m)	Alps	Switzerland
The Matterhorn	14,777 feet (4,479 m)	Alps	Switzerland/Italy
Mount Mulhacen	11,414 feet (3,479 m)	Sierra Nevada	Spain
Pico de Aneto	11,168 feet (3,404 m)	Pyrenees	Spain
Mount Etna	10,902 feet (3,323 m)	none	Italy (Sicily)
Mount Musala	9,596 feet (2,925 m)	Rila	Bulgaria
Gerlachovsky Peak	8,711 feet (2,655 m)	Carpathian	Slovakia

Mountains of Europe

Use the information on the other page and the map on this page to fill in the blanks.

1. The highest mountain in Europe is _____.

2. Europe's highest mountain is in the _____ range.

3. The highest mountain in the Carpathians is _____.

4. Mont Blanc is the _____ mountain in the Alps.

5. Three of Europe's largest rivers start in the _____.

6. Mount _____ in Sicily does not belong to a mountain range.

7. The Pyrenees separate the _____ Peninsula from the rest of Europe.

8. The _____ Mountains form the eastern edge of Europe.

9. Mount _____ in Bulgaria is 9,596 feet tall.

10. The tallest mountain in Spain is _____.

Volcanoes of Europe

Italy's Volcanoes

Most of Europe's active volcanoes are located in Italy. Mount Etna is located in Sicily and is the highest Italian mountain south of the Alps. The volcano is 10,922 feet (3,329 m) tall and covers 460 square miles (1,190 square km). Mount Etna began erupting about a half million years ago. Its most recent eruption was in 2010.

Mount Vesuvius is located in southern Italy, near the city of Naples. It is one of the most famous volcanoes in the world because of an eruption that happened in the year 79 AD. That eruption buried the cities of Pompeii and Herculaneum and killed between 10,000 and 25,000 people. Vesuvius has not erupted since 1944, but it could erupt again.

Mount Stromboli is located on a small island off the north coast of Sicily. It has erupted repeatedly for 2,000 years—and almost continuously since 1932. Stromboli is known for spectacular explosions of molten lava that make bright red arcs in the sky. Because its eruptions can be seen for long distances at night, Stromboli is called "the lighthouse of the Mediterranean."

Iceland's Volcanoes

Iceland was formed by a volcanic eruption millions of years ago, and the nation still has several active volcanoes. The most active volcano is Hekla, which towers 4,892 feet (1,491 m) over southern Iceland. This volcano has erupted several times over the past 100 years, most recently in the year 2000.

In 2010, an Icelandic volcano called Eyjafjallajökull sent clouds of volcanic ash into the skies over Iceland and Europe. The cloud was so thick that no planes could fly over Northern Europe for several days.

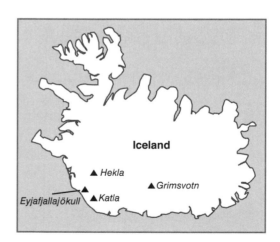

Volcanoes of Europe

Use the information and maps on the other page to help you complete the paragraphs about Italian and Icelandic volcanoes.

Three active volcanoes are located in the Southern European country of

_____. Probably the most famous of these volcanoes is

Mount _____, which destroyed two ancient cities in

79 AD. More than _____ people were killed as a result of

that eruption. The modern city of _____ is very close to

this volcano, which could _____ again.

On the island of Sicily, off the southern tip of Italy, is the 10,922-foot

Mount _____. This volcano has been erupting for a half

_____ years, most recently in _____.

Located off the coast of Sicily, the active volcano _____ has

been erupting for _____ years. It often sends bright red arcs

of _____ into the air.

There are also many volcanoes on the Northern European island of

_____. Its most active volcano is _____.

This volcano is about _____ feet tall, and its last eruption was

in _____. In 2010, a volcano named Eyjafjallajökull erupted, sending

out huge clouds of volcanic _____ over Europe. The clouds

were so thick that _____ were grounded for several days.

Europe's Forests

About 44% of Europe is covered by forest land. There are four main types of forest: boreal, temperate, Mediterranean, and mountain forests. These forests are expanding, mainly due to the planting of new trees.

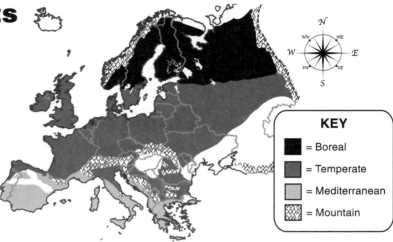

KEY

■ = Boreal
■ = Temperate
□ = Mediterranean
▨ = Mountain

Boreal Forests

Boreal forests can be found mostly in the northern countries of Sweden, Finland, and Russia. About three-quarters of the land in these countries is boreal forest land, which means it contains trees called *conifers*. These trees, which include pine, fir, and spruce trees, stay green all year. Conifers are able to survive long, cold winters and live in frozen soil. Broad-leaf birch trees, which are *deciduous* trees (trees that lose their leaves in the fall), are also found in the boreal forest.

Temperate Forests

Temperate forests are found in Northern and Western Europe, especially in Germany, Austria, and the UK. Temperate forests are home to a wide variety of trees, from the coniferous firs, spruces, and pines to the deciduous oak, beech, and chestnut trees. However, different trees in the temperate forest prefer different climates and terrains. Oak trees, which can be up to 131 feet (40 m) tall, grow on plains and hills. Beeches prefer cool, wet climates, such as those found in the mountains of France and Germany. Chestnut trees prefer warmer climates. Chestnuts can live for more than 1,500 years!

Mediterranean Forests

The countries of Spain, Portugal, Italy, and Greece, all of which border the Mediterranean Sea, have summers that are very hot and dry. Trees such as cork oak, maritime pine, eucalyptus, and chestnut are adapted to these conditions and make up the *Mediterranean forests*.

Mountain Forests

Mountain forests are found on the slopes of major mountain ranges such as the Alps. Different trees grow at each *tier*, or elevation level, of the mountain. Fir, beech, and larch trees grow on the lower tiers, while spruce, maple, and pine trees are common in the middle tiers. At the highest elevations, only shrub-sized fir trees survive.

Europe's Forests

A. Use the information on the other page to write the letter of the correct clue next to each term.

_____ 1. coniferous   a. a tree that can grow as a shrub at high elevations

_____ 2. deciduous   b. a deciduous tree that prefers cool, wet climates

_____ 3. oak   c. a term describing trees that stay green all year

_____ 4. beech   d. a country that has thick boreal forests

_____ 5. chestnut   e. an elevation level on a mountain

_____ 6. tier   f. a tree that grows in the Mediterranean forests

_____ 7. cork oak   g. a country where beeches grow

_____ 8. fir   h. a tree that can grow up to 131 feet high

_____ 9. Sweden   i. a deciduous tree that prefers warm climates

_____ 10. France   j. a term describing trees that grow new leaves every spring

B. Read each statement and circle the type of forest described. Use the information on the other page to help you.

1. Mostly conifers grow in this forest.   **boreal**   **temperate**

2. This type of forest grows in Northern and Western Europe.   **mountain**   **temperate**

3. The trees of this forest grow in hot and dry conditions.   **boreal**   **Mediterranean**

4. Trees in this forest grow in tiers.   **mountain**   **Mediterranean**

5. Italy has this type of forest.   **Mediterranean**   **temperate**

6. Birch trees are common in this forest.   **mountain**   **boreal**

7. Shrubby fir trees grow at the highest tiers of this forest.   **temperate**   **mountain**

Name _____

Northern Tundra

Parts of northern Russia, Finland, Iceland, Norway, and Sweden are covered in tundra. Tundra is an area where it is so cold that the soil from about 10 to 35 inches (25 to 90 cm) deep is frozen all year long. Only the top layer thaws out in the summer. The frozen ground underneath that layer is called *permafrost*.

During the winter, the temperature in this part of Europe can fall as low as –58°F (–50°C), with an average temperature of only about –18°F (–28°C). During the summer, temperatures rise to an average of about 54°F (12°C), which allows the top layer of soil to thaw out. This thawing makes the ground soggy, covering the tundra with marshes, bogs, lakes, and streams.

KEY

= Tundra

When the ground has thawed, some plants are able to grow. These include dwarf shrubs, grasses, mosses, and lichens (LIKE-enz). All of these plants are small, growing low and close to the ground. The permafrost prevents plants from developing a deep root system. Tundra plants only bloom for a few weeks, but during this time they turn the bare ground into a carpet of colorful flowers.

Although the European tundra is a harsh place, some people and animals do live there. A group of people called the Sami live in northern Sweden, Norway, Finland, and Russia. They are *nomadic*, meaning that they move from place to place so their reindeer herds can find plants to eat as the seasons change. Other animals such as lemmings, which are small rodents, also travel across the tundra, eating the plants that grow during the summer. Predators such as snowy owls and wolverines prey on the small mammals.

Name _____

Northern Tundra

A. Use the information and map on the other page to answer the questions.

1. What is the permanently frozen layer of the   _____
   tundra called?

2. During which season do plants grow in the tundra?   _____

3. What is tundra?

   _____

4. Which five countries have areas of tundra?

   _____

5. Name three animals that live in the tundra.

   _____

6. What is the tundra like in summer?

   _____

B. Read each statement. Circle **yes** if it is true or **no** if it is false. Use the information on the other page to help you.

1. In the winter, temperatures on the tundra can fall to –58°F.   **Yes**   **No**

2. Plants on the tundra must have deep root systems.   **Yes**   **No**

3. Tundra plants bloom in the spring.   **Yes**   **No**

4. Only the top layer of soil thaws during the summer.   **Yes**   **No**

5. In the summer, temperatures reach –54°F.   **Yes**   **No**

6. The ground on the tundra is covered with marshes during   **Yes**   **No**
   the summer.

7. Nomadic people herd lemmings across the tundra.   **Yes**   **No**

Europe's Bodies of Water

Two oceans border the continent of Europe. The frigid Arctic Ocean is to the north of Europe and the Atlantic Ocean is to the west. The circulating currents of the Atlantic Ocean, known as the Gulf Stream, are very important to Europe's climate. They help keep temperatures in Western and Southern Europe mild by bringing warm waters to the area.

Several major seas also surround Europe. The Norwegian and North seas border the Scandinavian Peninsula and the British Isles. In the south, the Mediterranean Sea and the Black Sea help separate Europe from Africa and Asia.

Other waterways help define Europe's coasts. The Strait of Gibraltar divides Spain from the African country of Morocco. The English Channel separates the UK from France. And the narrow Bosporus Strait helps connect the Black Sea to the Mediterranean Sea.

Within the continent of Europe, there are many important rivers. The Danube starts in Germany, flows across central Europe, and ends in the Black Sea. The Rhine flows through Switzerland, Germany, France, and the Netherlands, ending in the North Sea. The Thames (TEMZ) runs through England, and the Volga River flows 2,300 miles (3,700 km) through Russia before emptying into the Caspian Sea. Other important rivers include the Loire, Rhone, and Seine rivers in France, and the Po in Italy.

A. Find and circle the names of the bodies of water in the word puzzle. Words may appear across, down, or diagonally.

```
V A J G J L P I T Y W F E D C
O C D V S B L A C K Q U L I P
L E T A E E C N R U L P T G L
G B U E N Z C X B M N N E I P
A D F I U U A R U G A O R F O
K O E T K F B B L L A C K F E
R S M A L J Y E T X N O R T H
I E V N A U U A A L A D B V E
N M E D I T E R R A N E A N E
E N E L G D E R R O D E R N Q
H E Y A R C T I C S E A I K U
S B U B J L O T F I D H R E D
K C O S C A Y G I B R D H L T
E T H A M E S I C D G J R P X
```

Oceans:
Arctic
Atlantic

Seas:
Black
Mediterranean
North

Rivers:
Danube
Po
Rhine
Seine
Thames
Volga

Europe's Bodies of Water

B. Use blue to circle the names of all the oceans, seas, and rivers that were included in the word puzzle on the other page. Use red to circle the names of all the other bodies of water on the map. Then write a caption that includes at least two facts you learned about Europe's bodies of water.

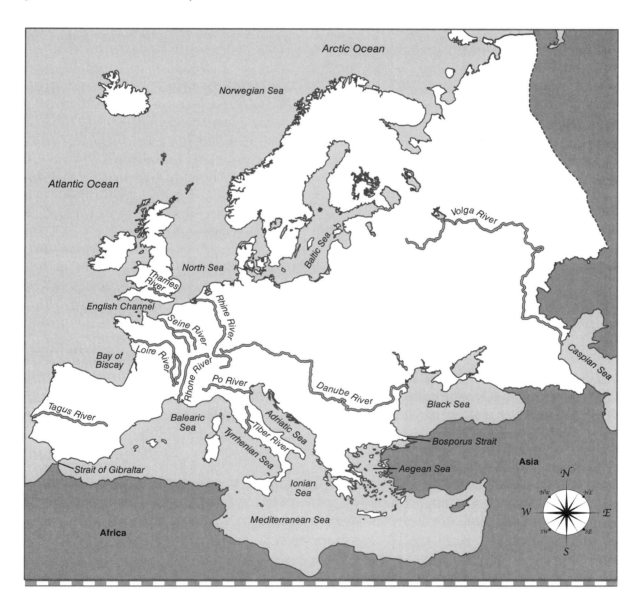

_____

_____

Seas of Europe

To the north and south, Europe is surrounded by seas, which are bodies of water partly or entirely enclosed by land. The cold seas of the north are connected to the Atlantic and Arctic oceans. The seas of the Mediterranean region are linked to the Atlantic Ocean by the Strait of Gibraltar.

The North Sea is located between the United Kingdom and northwestern Europe. It is a shallow sea with a depth of less than 150 feet (50 m) in some

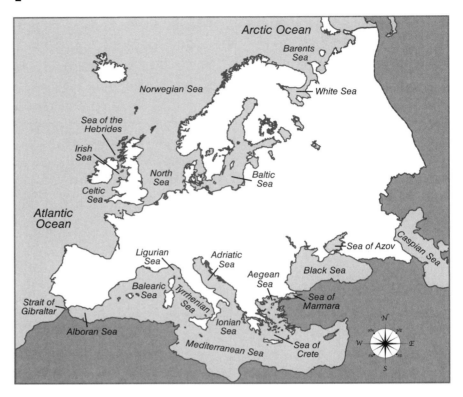

areas. This sea is one of the busiest shipping areas in the world.

The Norwegian Sea is northeast of the UK, between Norway and Iceland. Even though it is far north, the warm Gulf Stream currents keep it free of ice all year.

The Baltic Sea is almost totally surrounded by land. It is bordered by Sweden, Finland, Russia, Estonia, Latvia, Lithuania, Poland, Germany, and Denmark. Because it is almost completely separated from the ocean and has many rivers emptying into it, the Baltic is not very salty. It is even shallower than the North Sea and is quick to freeze in winter.

One of the most important seas in Southern Europe is the Mediterranean Sea. The Mediterranean Sea is almost completely surrounded by land. In fact, 21 countries have a coastline on the Mediterranean. Europe is to the north, Asia is to the east, and Africa is to the south of this large sea. The Mediterranean Sea is about 16,000 feet (4,900 m) deep in its deepest place and is one of Europe's saltier seas. A number of smaller seas are also part of the Mediterranean Sea, including the Adriatic, Aegean, Balearic, Ionian, and Tyrrhenian seas.

The Black Sea, which covers an area larger than Japan, is an inland sea located between southeastern Europe and western Asia. It is bordered by the European countries of Bulgaria, Romania, Ukraine, and Russia and the Asian countries of Turkey and Georgia. East of the Black Sea is the Caspian Sea, which also helps separate Europe from Asia.

Seas of Europe

Read each statement. Unscramble the answer and write it on the line.
Use the information and map on the other page to help you.

1. The _____ Sea is a busy shipping area.
   tohrn

2. The Strait of Gibraltar connects the Atlantic Ocean to the

   _____ Sea.
   tidenmearnare

3. The _____ Sea is located between Norway and Iceland.
   wergonina

4. The Mediterranean Sea contains many smaller seas, including the

   _____ Sea.
   tadiraci

5. The Mediterranean is an extremely _____ sea.
   tylsa

6. Part of the _____ Sea freezes over in the winter months.
   ciblat

7. The _____ Sea helps to separate Europe from Asia.
   kalcb

8. The seas in Northern Europe connect with the _____
   and Arctic oceans.   **caltanti**

9. The Mediterranean Sea is north of the continent of _____.
   farcia

10. The Black Sea is larger than the country of _____.
    pajna

11. The _____ Sea is east of the Black Sea.
    napsica

Rhine River

The Rhine River is the longest river in Germany and one of the longest rivers in Europe. It measures 765 miles (1,230 km) long. The Rhine begins at the Swiss Rheinwaldhorn Glacier in the Alps and flows along the border of Liechtenstein. It runs through Lake Constance before continuing through Switzerland and then turning north through Germany. Other large rivers, such as the Neckar, Main, and Moselle, join the Rhine along the way. Finally, the river empties into the North Sea in the Netherlands.

No other river in the world has so many old and famous cities on its banks, including Cologne, Germany, and Strasbourg, France. The middle part of the Rhine flows through the deep Rhine Gorge. Along this part of the river are more than 40 castles and fortresses that were built during the Middle Ages, as well as many vineyards and small country villages. Because of this, it is known as "the romantic Rhine."

The Rhine has been one of Europe's most important transport routes since the Roman Empire. About 540 miles (870 km) of its length can be traveled by ships. Many industries are located along the Rhine because it is cheaper to transport materials on water than on land. In fact, one-fifth of the world's chemical-making companies manufacture along the Rhine.

The amount of heavy industry along the Rhine has created severe pollution problems. In the 1970s and 1980s, the Rhine was called "the sewer of Europe." Since then, clean-up efforts have made the Rhine less polluted. A large number of fish have returned to the Rhine, and in some places, it is again possible to swim in the river.

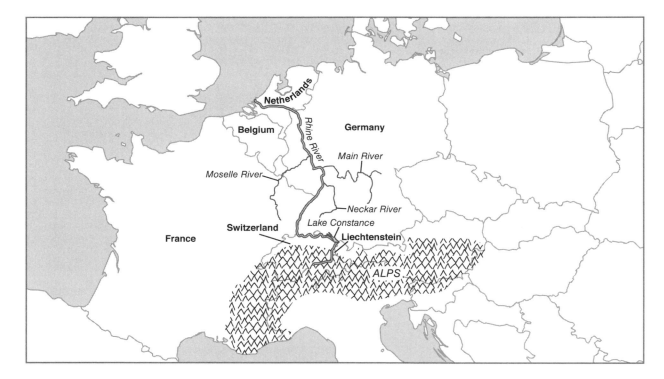

Rhine River

A. Write the letter of the clue that matches each name or number. Use the information and map on the other page to help you.

_____ 1. Alps

_____ 2. Rheinwaldhorn

_____ 3. Lake Constance

_____ 4. North Sea

_____ 5. 540 miles

_____ 6. 765 miles

_____ 7. Germany

_____ 8. Liechtenstein

_____ 9. Netherlands

a. the length of the Rhine

b. the sea where the Rhine ends

c. the tiny country that borders the Rhine near Switzerland

d. the length of the Rhine traveled by ships

e. the country where the Rhine ends

f. the glacier where the Rhine begins

g. the mountains where the Rhine begins

h. a lake fed by the Rhine

i. the Rhine travels through the western part of this country

B. Read each statement. Circle **yes** if it is true or **no** if it is false. Use the information and map on the other page to help you.

1. The Rhine is west of Belgium.   **Yes**   **No**

2. Old castles are seen along the Rhine.   **Yes**   **No**

3. Ships can navigate the entire length of the Rhine.   **Yes**   **No**

4. There is a lot of industry along the Rhine.   **Yes**   **No**

5. The Rhine flows through Lake Constance.   **Yes**   **No**

6. Water transport is cheaper than land transport.   **Yes**   **No**

7. The Rhine is less polluted now than in the last century.   **Yes**   **No**

8. The Rhine flows into the Black Sea.   **Yes**   **No**

Norway's Fjords

Fjords (FYORDS) are long, deep valleys cut between steep cliffs. These narrow gorges jut inland from the sea and are filled with salt water. Fjords were created long ago during ice ages, when glaciers moved across Earth, carving the land. Because glaciers move very slowly, it took more than 3 million years for the large chunks of ice to create Norway's fjords. The last ice age ended 10,000 years ago, at which time the fjords of Norway were fully formed.

The fjords in Norway are the most famous in the world. One of the best-known is Sognefjord (SAW-nyah-fyord), which is 125 miles (204 km) long and has both the

Geirangerfjord

deepest and widest points of any fjord in Norway. The water is 4,300 feet (1,300 m) deep at its deepest, and in one area, the fjord measures 2 miles (3 km) across.

Geirangerfjord (guy-RAHN-gheer-fyord) is farther north and has several tall waterfalls, including one named the Seven Sisters. Large cruise ships often sail into Geirangerfjord, and even these big ships look tiny when compared to the steep cliff walls.

Other fjords, such as Hardangerfjord (har-DON-gheer-fyord), are lined with green pastures and small villages.

Because of all the fjords, inlets, and bays along Norway's coast, the coastline is very jagged. In fact, if you stretched the coastline out flat, it would reach halfway around the world!

Norway's Fjords

A. Complete the sentences using information from the other page to help you.

1. Narrow coastal gorges with steep sides are called _____.

2. _____ is about 125 miles long.

3. The most famous fjords in the world are in _____.

4. The last ice age ended about _____ years ago.

5. Geirangerfjord has many tall _____, including the Seven Sisters.

6. If you flattened Norway's coastline, it would reach _____ around the world.

7. It took about _____ million years for the fjords to form.

8. _____ is a fjord lined with green pastures and villages.

9. Fjords were created by moving _____ during the Ice Age.

10. _____ has both the deepest and widest points of any fjord in Norway.

B. Write three facts about Norway's fjords that are not mentioned in the activity above. Use the information and map on the other page to help you.

1. _____

2. _____

3. _____

Review

Use words from the box to complete the crossword puzzle.

Balkan

conifers

fjords

Mediterranean

Rhine

tundra

volcanoes

Across

3. Norway has many _____.

5. The _____ River is the longest river in Germany.

6. The soil is nearly always frozen in the _____.

7. The _____ Peninsula is located in southeastern Europe.

Down

1. Italy and Iceland have many _____.

2. The _____ Sea borders Europe to the south.

4. Forests filled with _____ are common in Northern Europe.

Valuable Resources of Europe

This section introduces students to the natural resources of Europe. Students discover that areas of the North Sea and Russia are large oil-producing regions. Students also learn that timber is an important resource, especially in Russia and the countries of Northern Europe, as are fish from Europe's seas and waterways. Students find out that corn, wheat, and potatoes are farmed in Europe, and that the vineyards of Southern Europe produce some of the world's largest supplies of grapes and wine. Finally, students become familiar with important wild and domesticated animals of Europe.

Each skill in this section is based on the following National Geography Standards:

Essential Element 3: Physical Systems

Standard 8: The characteristics and spatial distribution of ecosystems on Earth's surface

Essential Element 5: Environment and Society

Standard 14: How human actions modify the physical environment

Standard 16: The changes that occur in the meaning, use, distribution, and importance of resources

CONTENTS

Overview

Natural resources are the minerals, plants, animals, and other elements that humans use from their environment. Europe is rich in many kinds of natural resources. There are large deposits of oil and coal, as well as a thriving fishing and farming industry. The abundant forests of Europe provide people with timber, and wild animals with a home.

Oil and Coal

Both oil and coal are important resources in Europe. They are *fossil fuels,* taking millions of years to form. Earth has only a limited supply of both of these sources of energy.

Europe contains several oil-producing regions, including the North Sea, Russia, Romania, Bulgaria, Ukraine, Austria, and Germany. Coal is mined in parts of Russia, Germany, and Ukraine, as well as in Poland.

Fishing and Farming

Fishing is a big business in Europe. Many kinds of fish and shellfish are caught in the North Sea, Mediterranean Sea, and other bodies of water. Cod, tuna, salmon, and haddock are some examples of the hundreds of types of seafood caught.

Farming is another important industry in Europe. The large, flat plains of Russia, Germany, France, and the United Kingdom are well-suited for growing crops such as potatoes, wheat, and corn. The warm climate of Italy and other countries on the Mediterranean Sea is ideal for growing grapes and olives.

Forests of Europe

Although many of Europe's forests have been cut down over the years, the continent's forests are now growing and provide a large amount of timber. The wood from these forests is used to make houses, furniture, and other building materials. Forests also provide homes to Europe's wild animals.

Wild and Domesticated Animals

Elk, reindeer, and moose are some of the largest wild animals living in Europe. The continent is also home to many smaller animals, such as foxes, rabbits, eagles, and badgers.

Livestock provide valuable resources for Europeans, who raise cattle, sheep, pigs, and reindeer for their dairy products, meat, wool, and hides.

Overview

Fill in the bubble to answer each question.

1. Which country is a top producer of coal?
   - Ⓐ United Kingdom
   - Ⓑ Germany
   - Ⓒ Italy
   - Ⓓ Greece

2. Which area is a top producer of oil?
   - Ⓐ North Sea
   - Ⓑ Adriatic Sea
   - Ⓒ Mediterranean Sea
   - Ⓓ Black Sea

3. Europe's large, open plains are well-suited for growing which crop?
   - Ⓐ cod
   - Ⓑ rice
   - Ⓒ wheat
   - Ⓓ timber

4. Which feature of Italy is ideal for growing grapes?
   - Ⓐ its mountains
   - Ⓑ its forests
   - Ⓒ its warm climate
   - Ⓓ its flat plains

5. Which of these is a small wild animal that lives in Europe's forests?
   - Ⓐ reindeer
   - Ⓑ fox
   - Ⓒ pig
   - Ⓓ moose

Oil Production in Europe

Oil is a fossil fuel. This means that it was formed from the remains of animals and plants that lived millions of years ago. These remains were covered by layers of soil. Over time, heat and pressure turned the remains into what is called *crude oil*.

Crude oil is a yellowish-black liquid that is usually found in underground reservoirs. A well is drilled into the reservoir to bring the crude oil to the surface. The oil is then sent to a refinery, or factory, where it is separated into usable products such as gasoline, diesel fuel, and heating oil. Crude oil is often called "black gold" because it is very valuable. It provides much of the world's fuel supply, it is expensive to produce, and takes so long to form that there is only a limited supply of it on Earth.

European countries produce about 18% of the world's crude oil. Russia accounts for over two-thirds of this oil. However, most of Russia's oil is produced east of the Ural Mountains, in Asia. In addition to Russia, the 10 highest oil-producing countries in Europe are Norway, the UK, Denmark, Germany, Italy, Romania, Ukraine, the Netherlands, and France.

While most of the oil produced in Europe comes from *onshore* wells, or wells drilled on dry land, over one-quarter comes from deepwater wells in the North Sea. Major oil production started in the North Sea in the 1940s and took off during the 1960s and 1970s as more oil reserves were found. Today, four countries—Norway, the United Kingdom, Denmark, and the Netherlands—produce oil from this sea. Norway controls over half of the North Sea's oil reserves.

The future of drilling for oil in the North Sea is in question. Production has declined since 2000. One reason is that no new oil fields have been discovered, while older ones are drying up. Another factor may be the 2010 oil spill off the coast of Louisiana in the United States. The spill was caused by a deepwater drilling rig that exploded, gushing oil from 5,000 feet below the ocean surface. It was the largest oil spill ever, with extensive damage to wildlife, fishing, and tourism. In reaction to this spill, Norway banned new deepwater drilling in the North Sea.

The North Sea's Top Oil-Producing Countries
one barrel = 42 gallons (159 liters)

	Country	Barrels Produced Each Day
1	Norway	2,350,000
2	United Kingdom	1,422,000
3	Denmark	262,000
4	The Netherlands	25,564

2009 Statistics from Energy Information Administration

Oil Production in Europe

A. Read each statement. Circle **yes** if it is true or **no** if it is false. Use the information on the other page to help you.

1. There is a limitless supply of crude oil.   **Yes   No**

2. Norway produces more than 2,000,000 barrels of oil per day.   **Yes   No**

3. The United Kingdom is the top oil producer in the North Sea.   **Yes   No**

4. Oil is found in underground reservoirs.   **Yes   No**

5. Denmark ranks third in North Sea oil production.   **Yes   No**

6. The Netherlands produces the least amount of oil in the North Sea.   **Yes   No**

7. European Russia produces 18% of the world's oil.   **Yes   No**

8. In 2010, an explosion caused a devastating oil spill in the North Sea.   **Yes   No**

9. Oil production in the North Sea is increasing.   **Yes   No**

10. Crude oil is used to make gasoline, diesel fuel, and heating oil.   **Yes   No**

B. Norway produces about 2,350,000 barrels of oil per day. One barrel equals 42 gallons, or 159 liters. Use this information and your math skills to answer the three questions below. Circle the correct answer.

1. About how many gallons of oil does Norway produce per day?

   987 gallons   987,000,000 gallons   98,700,000 gallons

2. About how many liters of oil does Norway produce per day?

   373,650 liters   37,365,000 liters   373,650,000 liters

3. How does a gallon of oil compare to a liter?

   **a gallon is about 4 times   a liter is about 4 times
   larger than a liter   larger than a gallon**

Fishing in Europe

The continent of Europe is surrounded by water on three sides. Most of the countries of Europe border an ocean or sea. So it is no surprise that nearly 800,000 Europeans are involved in the fishing industry.

Wild Capture

Each year, over 13 million metric tons of wild fish are caught by the commercial fishing industry in Europe. The countries that catch the largest amounts of fish are Russia, with 3.3 million metric tons, and Norway, with 2.3 million metric tons. The third-largest fishing industry is in Iceland, where nearly 1.3 million metric tons are caught each year. Rounding out the top five European fishing countries are Spain and Denmark.

Large fish such as cod, tuna, salmon, and haddock are caught in the Atlantic Ocean, Mediterranean Sea, and North Sea. Millions of smaller fish, such as anchovies, herring, and sardines, are also fished from coastal waters.

Europe's fishing industry, however, faces many challenges today. Overfishing has caused many types of fish to disappear. Some species, including the bluefin tuna, which is found in the Atlantic Ocean and Mediterranean Sea, are in danger of dying out completely. Efforts are underway to limit the number of bluefin tuna that can be caught each year and to make some areas off-limits to tuna fishing altogether. Officials hope that these efforts will allow the tuna population to increase so that people can once again catch these fish without endangering the species.

In addition, fishing fleets are looking for better ways to catch fish without harming other species, such as dolphins. Large numbers of dolphins and other marine life are often trapped and killed in fishing nets by mistake.

Aquaculture

Not all fish are captured in the wild. Many are raised on fish farms. Raising fish this way is called *aquaculture*. The most common fish and shellfish farmed in Europe are salmon, trout, and mussels. As commercial fishing in the wild becomes more difficult, aquaculture will become more important.

The largest aquaculture industry in Europe is in Norway, which produces almost three times the amount of farmed fish as its closest competitor, Spain. Other European countries with large aquaculture industries are France, the United Kingdom, Italy, and Greece. Farmed fish are not only eaten by Europeans, but they are also exported to other countries around the world.

Fishing in Europe

A. Use the information on the other page to complete the paragraphs on fishing in Europe.

    Because most countries in Europe border an ocean or a sea,

_____ fishing is a huge industry for Europeans. More

than 13 million metric _____ of fish are caught each

year. _____ is the country that catches the most fish,

followed by Norway and _____.

    The fishing industry faces many challenges because of overfishing. This

practice has caused species such as the bluefin _____ to

become endangered. In order to prevent overfishing, many fish are farm raised.

The most common European farmed fish are _____,

trout, and mussels. The country of _____ has the

largest aquaculture industry in Europe.

B. Write three facts about fishing in Europe using information from the other page.

1. _____

   _____

2. _____

   _____

3. _____

   _____

Europe's Grains and Potatoes

Grains

Wheat, corn, and oats are grain crops commonly grown in Europe. They serve as important sources of food for the people and animals of Europe, as well as for exporting to other places in the world.

Wheat is the most important grain crop in Europe. It is grown in Russia, Germany, Romania, France, Poland, Italy, Spain, and the United Kingdom. Wheat accounts for about 30% of the food calories consumed in Russia and the rest of Eastern Europe. Wheat can be made into a variety of foods, including bread, pasta, cereal, and cookies. These foods are popular in Europe and around the world. Italy is especially well-known for its various types of fine wheat pastas.

Corn is another valuable grain crop. France, Romania, Hungary, and Ukraine are all major corn producers. Like wheat, corn is ground into flour and used to make bread. It is also eaten fresh, canned, or frozen.

Oats need a cool, moist climate to grow. Russia, Finland, Sweden, and Scotland are all major producers of oats. A large percentage of oats are used to feed cattle. But oats are also used to make bread, cereal, and oatmeal.

Potatoes

Potatoes are plants with an edible part called a *tuber*, which grows underground. Potatoes were first grown in Peru about 10,000 years ago. Spanish sailors brought potatoes back to Europe in the 1550s. Russia, Ukraine, and Germany are the largest potato producers in Europe.

Fast Facts About Potatoes

- The English word *potato* comes from the Spanish word *patata*.

- An average person in the European country of Belarus eats about 2 pounds (0.9 kg) of potatoes a day.

- Potatoes grow best in a cool, damp climate.

- Potatoes are a great source of vitamins and minerals, especially vitamin C and potassium.

- Many Irish people immigrated to the United States and Canada in the 1800s when a disease called *blight* destroyed most of the potato crop in Ireland.

- There are about 4,000 different varieties of potatoes. Some of the most popular ones are russet, red bliss, and yukon gold potatoes.

Europe's Grains and Potatoes

A. Write the letter of the clue that matches each word or number related to potatoes. Use the information on the other page to help you.

_____ 1. 4,000

_____ 2. Belarus

_____ 3. sailors

_____ 4. Peru

_____ 5. potassium

_____ 6. Germany

_____ 7. 10,000

_____ 8. tuber

_____ 9. patata

_____ 10. blight

a. the country where potatoes were first grown

b. the number of years ago potatoes were first grown

c. the Spanish word meaning *potato*

d. a disease that affects potatoes

e. the country where each person eats about 2 pounds of potatoes a day

f. people who brought potatoes to Europe

g. a country that produces a lot of potatoes

h. the number of potato varieties

i. a nutrient found in potatoes

j. the edible part of a potato plant

B. Use the information on the other page to complete the sentences.

1. Ground _____ is the main ingredient in many Italian pastas.

2. Grains are _____ from Europe to countries around the world.

3. About 30% of the _____ consumed in Eastern Europe come from foods made from wheat.

4. _____ that is grown in Europe is often canned, frozen, or ground into flour.

5. Finland and Scotland are major producers of _____.

6. _____ is a type of hot cereal made from oats.

Olives of the Mediterranean

Olive trees are native to the coastal areas of the Mediterranean Sea, where the climate is warm year-round. There are more than 750 million olive trees in the world, and almost all of them grow near the Mediterranean. These trees grow between 25 and 50 feet (8 to 15 m) tall. They have thick, ropy trunks and long, silvery-green leaves.

Olive trees can live a long time. Some trees in Italy are said to date back thousands of years to the days of ancient Rome. Other trees in Greece and Montenegro are said to be 2,000 years old.

olive tree

Olives, the fruit of olive trees, have been harvested in Europe for thousands of years. There are many varieties, such as the dark purple, almond-shaped kalamata olive from Greece and the common green manzanilla olive from Spain.

Olives and olive oil have many uses. People eat olives in salads or as snacks. Olive pits are often removed, and the olives are stuffed with everything from garlic to cheese. Olives can also be mashed and used as a spread for bread. The oil from olives is used for cooking or as a dressing for salads. Olive oil is also put into skincare products, and the wood from olive trees can be used to build furniture.

Olives are a big business in Europe. Spain, Italy, Greece, and Portugal are Europe's biggest producers of olives and olive oil. Greece produces more black olives than any other country and also has more varieties of olives than any other nation. In fact, about 60% of the farmland in Greece is used to grow olives.

Three European countries produce more than half of all the olive oil in the world. Spain produces about 40% of the world's olive oil, with Italy coming in second and Greece at number three. Portugal also produces small amounts of olive oil.

European countries not only make a lot of olive oil, they also consume high percentages of it compared to the rest of the world. Italy consumes about 30% of the olive oil in the world, while Spain eats about 20% of the world's supply.

Olives of the Mediterranean

A. Circle the word that completes each sentence. Use the information on the other page to help you.

1. Olives have been grown for ＿＿ of years.   **thousands**   **millions**

2. There are over 750 million olive trees in ＿＿.   **Europe**   **the world**

3. Olive oil is used to make ＿＿.   **skin products**   **furniture**

4. Olive trees can be up to 50 ＿＿ tall.   **feet**   **meters**

5. The manzanilla olive from Spain is ＿＿.   **purple**   **green**

6. Some olive trees in ＿＿ may be more than 2,000 years old.   **Portugal**   **Greece**

7. Olive trees have silvery-green ＿＿.   **trunks**   **leaves**

8. About 60% of the farmland in ＿＿ is used to grow olives.   **Greece**   **Spain**

9. ＿＿ produces about 40% of the world's olive oil.   **Portugal**   **Spain**

10. People in ＿＿ eat more olive oil than anywhere else in the world.   **Italy**   **Turkey**

B. Use the information on the other page to write a sentence about where olives are grown in Europe.

_____

_____

_____

Wine Production in Europe

Winemaking is an important industry in Europe. Every European country except Estonia produces some amount of wine. In 2008, Italy surpassed France as the largest producer of wine in the world. Together, Italy and France produce about 34% of the world's wine, much of which is exported. Spain, Germany, and Portugal complete the top five wine-producing countries of Europe, in that order.

The three European countries with the most land devoted to growing grapes for winemaking are Spain, France, and Italy. Lands where grapes grow are called *vineyards*. Vineyards have existed in Europe for thousands of years. Many vineyards are located on hillsides where the soil is not good for growing other crops. In fact, some kinds of grapes actually thrive in poor, rocky soils.

The process of making wine begins when the grapes are *harvested*, or picked, from the vines between August and October. Harvesting can be done by hand or by machine. The grapes are then pressed so that all the juice runs out. Yeast is added to the grape juice to *ferment* it, or turn the sugars in the grapes into alcohol. The wine is then placed in a bottle and stored for at least a year until it is ready to drink.

While Italy produces more wine than any other country, France has long set the standard for wines around the world. French wines, which can be very expensive, are prized by people who appreciate fine wines. Most of the great grapes grown around the world for winemaking come from grapevines that were originally imported from France. French people drink more wine than the people of any other European country.

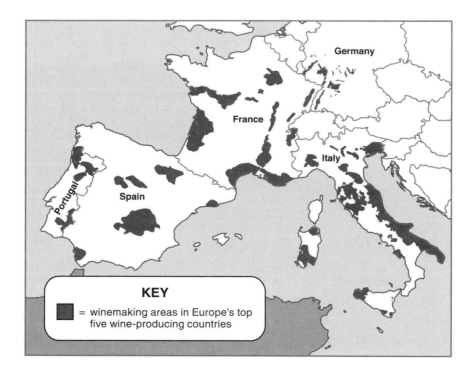

KEY

■ = winemaking areas in Europe's top five wine-producing countries

Wine Production in Europe

A. Use the information on the other page to answer the questions.

1. Which country produces the most wine in the world? _____

2. What three European countries grow the most grapes?

    _____

3. Why are vineyards often planted on hillsides?

    _____

    _____

4. Describe the steps in the winemaking process, from harvest to bottling.

    _____

    _____

    _____

    _____

B. Use the information and map on the other page to rank Europe's top five wine producers from largest to smallest. On the map, lightly shade each country in the correct color.

Rank	Country	Color
1		green
2		red
3		yellow
4		orange
5		brown

Europe's Livestock

Animals that are raised for food or to provide other products or services to people are called *livestock*. Examples of livestock in Europe are cattle, sheep, reindeer, goats, and pigs. Livestock have many uses, including providing meat and dairy products. The wool and hides of the animals are used to make clothes, blankets, and leather goods. Livestock can also be used for labor.

Cattle

The term *cattle* includes oxen, bulls, and cows. Oxen and bulls are male animals, while cows are female. There are about 130 million cattle in Europe today. Although male and female cattle are both raised for their meat, oxen are typically used for farm labor, while cows are prized for the milk they produce.

Cows that are used for milk production are called dairy cows. The milk produced by cows is a valuable food source because it can be processed into dairy products such as butter, yogurt, and cheese. Cheese is an especially popular dairy product in Europe. Different regions of Europe produce cheese with distinct flavors. These cheeses are exported all over the world. Germany and France are the leading European producers of cheese.

Sheep

Spain, the United Kingdom, Ireland, Portugal, and the Netherlands all have large sheep populations, which require large areas of pasture to survive. A sheep's thick fleece is cut off every year and woven into wool, which can be made into everything from sweaters to blankets. Sheep are also valued for their meat, which is called *mutton*. In addition, sheep's milk can be used to make cheese.

Pigs

Pigs are raised for their meat and provide a valuable food source for Europe's population, as well as for export to other parts of the world. Pig meat, or *pork,* can be made into pork chops, loin, spareribs, and bacon. Pork can also be used to make many types of sausages, including the famous German bratwurst and Polish kielbasa. Belgium, Spain, and the Netherlands raise the largest number of pigs in Europe.

Reindeer

Reindeer are an important resource to people who live in Northern Europe. These animals are often used to pull sleds over the snowy landscape. In Norway, the Sami people herd reindeer and use them for their milk, meat, and skins.

Europe's Livestock

A. Read each statement. Circle **yes** if it is true or **no** if it is false. Use the information on the other page to help you.

1. Livestock include pets such as dogs and cats.   **Yes   No**

2. German bratwurst is made from sheep's meat.   **Yes   No**

3. Bacon, sausage, and spareribs are made from pork.   **Yes   No**

4. Oxen are valued for the milk they produce.   **Yes   No**

5. Reindeer are prized for their milk, meat, and skins.   **Yes   No**

6. Mutton is a valuable resource that comes from sheep.   **Yes   No**

7. Belgium has the largest sheep population in Europe.   **Yes   No**

8. Reindeer are found only in Southern Europe.   **Yes   No**

9. The Sami are a group of people who herd reindeer.   **Yes   No**

10. Italy is the number one producer of cheese in Europe.   **Yes   No**

B. Choose three animals from the other page and write a sentence about each one. Describe why each animal is an important resource for Europeans.

1. _____

_____

2. _____

_____

3. _____

_____

Europe's Forests

Forests are an important natural resource in Europe for several reasons. Forests provide *timber*, or wood that can be used for building and to make paper and other products. Forests also provide a home for wild animals and plants. Perhaps most importantly, the trees produce oxygen that helps support all life on Earth.

The Importance of Timber

People have been using timber from forests for thousands of years. Some trees, such as firs and oaks, provide strong wood that is good for construction. Other trees, such as the hemlock, produce a softer wood that can be used for cardboard. Here are a few of Europe's trees and how their timber is used:

Type of Tree	Uses
Beech	furniture, flooring, musical instruments
Cork Oak	bottle corks, flooring
Elm	furniture, docks and piers
Horse Chestnut	beams for construction
Larch	fences
Willow	baskets, toys

A Home for Animals

Forests provide homes for another important European resource: wild animals. Foxes, deer, rabbits, weasels, and squirrels live in Europe's temperate forests. Moose and elk live in the boreal forests of Northern Europe. Europe's forests are also home to reptiles and amphibians such as snakes, frogs, and salamanders. Songbirds and birds of prey, such as hawks and owls, live and find food in forests.

Saving Europe's Forests

Even though Europe has a lot of forests, they face many dangers. Millions of trees have been cut down not just for their timber, but to clear land for housing developments, shopping malls, and highways. Another big danger to Europe's forests is pollution. Millions of acres of forests have been killed or damaged by *acid rain*, which is rain that contains chemicals from factories and other air pollutants.

Many people are trying to save Europe's forests. Scientists and government officials are creating plans to reduce pollution and the cutting down of trees. And some forests have been preserved as national parks, such as the New Forest in the United Kingdom and the Foreste Casentinesi in Italy. There, the trees and animals that the forests shelter can remain undisturbed.

Europe's Forests

A. Use the information on the other page to answer the questions.

1. What is timber?

   _____

2. Write three reasons why forests are important.

   _____

   _____

   _____

3. Name two threats to European forests.

   _____

   _____

4. How can the people of Europe help save their forests?

   _____

   _____

B. List four types of trees used for timber in Europe. Then name one way each tree is used.

Tree	Use
_____	_____
_____	_____
_____	_____
_____	_____

Wildlife of Europe

Badger

The badger belongs to the weasel family and thrives throughout Europe.

Habitat
- forests of central Europe
- lives in underground homes called *setts*

Characteristics
- gray with black-and-white striped head
- weighs 22–44 lbs (10–20 kg)
- strong legs and sharp claws

Diet
- favorite foods are earthworms, fruit, nuts, and birds' eggs
- eats wasp and bee larvae

Reproduction
- female gives birth to one to five cubs after a seven-week pregnancy
- newborn cubs are blind and covered with light, silky hair

Behavior
- nocturnal (active at night)
- lives in large family groups

Enemies
- foxes, eagles, wolves, lynxes, humans

Status
- common; population is increasing

Barbary Macaque

Barbary macaques are the only monkeys living in the wild in Europe today.

Habitat
- Rock of Gibraltar, near Spain
- lives in cedar and oak forests

Characteristics
- covered with yellow-brown hair
- weighs up to 24 lbs (11 kg)

Diet
- fruit, roots, leaves, insects

Reproduction
- female gives birth to one baby after a six-month pregnancy
- newborn babies weigh about 1 lb (450 grams)

Behavior
- active during the day
- lives in large groups
- sleeps in trees at night

Enemies
- humans

Status
- endangered; the population has declined by as much as 50% over the last 25 years

Wildlife of Europe

Iberian Lynx

This predator is the most endangered cat species in the world due to habitat loss.

Habitat
• open scrublands of Portugal and Spain

Characteristics
• weighs 20–30 lbs (9–13 kg)
• brown, white, and black fur with spots
• tufts of fur at the top of each ear and on cheeks
• bobbed (short) tail

Diet
• mostly rabbits

Reproduction
• female gives birth to two or three kittens
• pregnancy lasts about two months
• kittens are blind and helpless when born

Behavior
• adult lives alone; mothers and kittens live together
• nocturnal (active at night)

Enemies
• humans

Status
• critically endangered; only about 85–150 animals are left in the wild

Hermann's Tortoise

This small, colorful tortoise is threatened by habitat loss and the pet trade.

Habitat
• Southern Europe, including Italy, the Balkans, Bulgaria, and some Greek islands
• lives in forests and meadows

Characteristics
• has a yellow and black *carapace*, or shell
• weighs 6–9 lbs (3–4 kg)
• has a hooked upper jaw

Diet
• leaves, flowers, fruit

Reproduction
• female lays two to three eggs in a *clutch*, or batch
• may lay several clutches each year
• hatchlings can care for themselves

Behavior
• lives alone for up to 75 years in the wild

Enemies
• humans

Status
• threatened; population is declining in some areas, but stable in the Balkans

Wildlife of Europe

Red Fox

This fox is the most widespread and abundant species of fox in the world.

Habitat
• lives in nearly every country in Europe

Characteristics
• long, silky red fur and bushy tail
• almond-shaped eyes set above a narrow snout
• 12–21 inches (31–56 cm) long
• weighs 6–24 lbs (3–11 kg)

Diet
• mice, insects, birds' eggs, fruit
• buries food to save for later

Reproduction
• female gives birth to four kits after a two-month pregnancy
• kits are born in the spring

Behavior
• mates for life
• a good swimmer and jumper
• can run up to 30 miles (48 kg) per hour

Enemies
• wolves, lynxes, bears, humans

Status
• common; populations are stable throughout the Northern Hemisphere

Osprey

This bird is one of the world's most powerful predators.

Habitat
• boreal forests of Northern Europe
• lives near water

Characteristics
• wingspan can reach more than 5 feet (1.5 m) across
• weighs about 4 lbs (2 kg)
• long, spiked claws

Diet
• fish scooped out of lakes

Reproduction
• female lays three eggs
• chicks stay in the nest for about eight weeks

Behavior
• builds huge nests called *eyries*
• migrates to Africa during the winter

Enemies
• eagle-owls, humans

Status
• common; populations can be found on all continents except Antarctica

Name _____

Wildlife of Europe

A. Read each characteristic and then write the name of the animal it describes. Use the animals listed in the box and the information on the other pages to help you.

> osprey   Iberian lynx   Hermann's tortoise
>
> red fox   badger   Barbary macaque

1. lives in the scrublands of Portugal and Spain   _____

2. can run up to 30 miles an hour   _____

3. the only wild monkey in Europe   _____

4. foxes and eagles are two of its enemies   _____

5. can live up to 75 years   _____

6. mates for life   _____

7. catches fish with its sharp claws   _____

8. has a bobbed tail and tufted ears   _____

9. lives near water in the boreal forests   _____

10. sleeps in trees at night   _____

11. has a carapace   _____

12. lives in underground homes called setts   _____

B. Which of the wild animals of Europe would you like to learn more about? Why?

_____

_____

_____

Review

Use words from the box to complete the crossword puzzle.

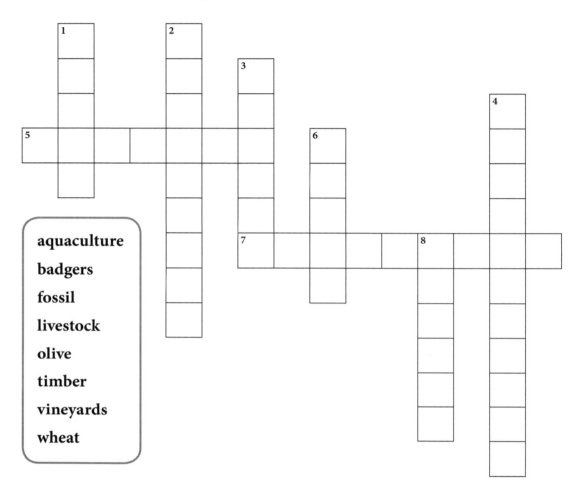

aquaculture

badgers

fossil

livestock

olive

timber

vineyards

wheat

Across

5. ____ and ospreys live in Europe's forests.

7. European ____ includes cattle, sheep, and pigs.

Down

1. ____ is the most common crop grown in Europe.

2. Grapes grow in ____ throughout Europe.

3. Crude oil is a ____ fuel.

4. Raising fish on farms is called ____.

6. Spain produces 40% of the world's ____ oil.

8. European forests provide ____ for building.

European Culture

This section introduces students to the architecture, arts, beliefs, and traditions of Europe. Students study six major tourist attractions in Europe and discover Europe's rich history of art, music, and dance. They also study the major religions of Europe and take a look at different types of European cuisine. Finally, students learn about the Running of the Bulls in Spain and Oktoberfest in Germany.

Each skill in this section is based on the following National Geography Standards:

Essential Element 2: Places and Regions

Standard 6: How culture and experience influence people's perceptions of places and regions

Essential Element 4: Human Systems

Standard 10: The characteristics, distribution, and complexity of Earth's cultural mosaics

CONTENTS

Overview

The *culture* of a group of people consists of their beliefs, customs, and traditions. Culture is displayed in people's artwork, literature, language, and architecture. The rich diversity of European culture reflects the various groups that live on the continent.

Tourist Attractions

Many world-famous historic and cultural attractions are found in Europe. Popular attractions include the Eiffel Tower in France, the Colosseum in Rome, the Parthenon in Greece, Big Ben in London, St. Basil's Cathedral in Moscow, and the Alhambra in Spain.

Arts and Entertainment

Europe boasts a long history of achievement in music, art, and dance. Italian artists created a rich heritage of fine art and sculpture during the Renaissance period. Europe's musical contributions range from classical composers such as Johann Sebastian Bach to legendary rock-and-roll artists such as The Beatles. Europe was also the birthplace of ballet.

Major Religions

People in Europe practice a wide variety of religions, including Catholicism, Judaism, Hinduism, and Islam. Protestantism, a type of Christian religion, began in Germany.

Sports

A number of sports are popular in Europe. The continent's most popular sport is soccer (called *football* in Europe and on other continents), but other sports such as rugby, cricket, and golf have a huge following as well.

Cuisine

The diverse foods of Europe have influenced dining all over the world. Popular foods such as pizza, paella, goulash, and Belgian waffles originated in Europe.

Celebrations

Every country in Europe has its own special holidays and celebrations. Oktoberfest is a celebration of the harvest that is observed in Germany, while Spain's Running of the Bulls has expanded from a local celebration to one that gets worldwide attention.

Overview

Fill in the bubble to answer each question or complete each sentence.

1. Oktoberfest is a festival held in _____.
   Ⓐ Spain
   Ⓑ Germany
   Ⓒ the United Kingdom
   Ⓓ Russia

2. The Eiffel Tower is located in which country?
   Ⓐ Italy
   Ⓑ Greece
   Ⓒ France
   Ⓓ Russia

3. Which religion originated in Germany?
   Ⓐ Protestantism
   Ⓑ Catholicism
   Ⓒ Judaism
   Ⓓ Islam

4. Which food is *not* mentioned as coming from Europe?
   Ⓐ sushi
   Ⓑ goulash
   Ⓒ pizza
   Ⓓ paella

5. Which is the most popular sport in Europe?
   Ⓐ rugby
   Ⓑ cricket
   Ⓒ basketball
   Ⓓ soccer

Tourist Attractions

Europe is a continent filled with amazing cultural and historic sites. Millions of tourists from all over the world travel to see these sites each year. Here are a few of Europe's most well-known tourist attractions.

The Eiffel Tower

The Eiffel Tower is located in Paris, France. The tower was built in 1889 for a festival called the Paris Exhibition and was named after the engineer who designed the structure, Alexandre Gustave Eiffel. The Eiffel Tower is 1,063 feet (324 m) tall, including an antenna on top that was later used for radio and television broadcasts. When the tower was built, it was the tallest structure in the world. It held that record until the Chrysler Building in New York City was erected about 40 years later.

Although the Eiffel Tower is a symbol of France today, not everyone was excited about the tower when it was being built. Several famous writers and artists signed a petition against erecting the tower because they thought it was a useless monstrosity. Some nature lovers worried that such a tall tower would cause trouble for birds flying over Paris. Despite these protests, the Eiffel Tower was built and became one of France's most popular and recognizable tourist attractions.

The Colosseum

The Colosseum, a huge stadium built about 2,000 years ago, may be the most famous landmark in Rome. It was built by the emperor Vespasian to provide a place for Romans to enjoy large spectacles. It could seat 50,000 people and had nearly 80 entrances so that crowds could enter and exit quickly. Seating was divided into three *tiers*, or levels. In the lowest tier with the best view sat the emperor, important priests, and government officials called *senators*. In the next tier sat members of the upper class. Ordinary citizens sat in the third tier, closer to the top of the stadium.

Romans came to the Colosseum to see exciting events, including contests in which men tried to kill wild animals and gladiators battled each other to the death. The Colosseum was even flooded with water to stage mock sea battles!

The Colosseum was abandoned around 520 AD. In the 18th century, Pope Benedict XIV declared the Colosseum a holy ground because so many Christians had been killed there. Since then, the site has been excavated by archaeologists and parts of it have been restored. The Colosseum is a top tourist attraction in Rome today.

Tourist Attractions

The Parthenon

The Parthenon was built in Athens, Greece, between the years 447 and 432 BC. It was a temple dedicated to the Greek goddess Athena. Inside the temple was a giant gold and ivory statue of the goddess that is no longer there today.

The Parthenon is located on a hill called the Acropolis, and it can be seen from many places in the city. The temple features eight columns across the front and back and seventeen columns along each side. About 13,400 stone blocks were used to build the structure. Builders used precise mathematical formulas to design the Parthenon in order to make sure that the building would last a long time. They did a good job, because visitors can still see the structure today, thousands of years after it was built.

Big Ben

For more than 150 years, visitors to London have admired the beautiful clock tower that rises above the Thames River. The tower stands over the Houses of Parliament, which are the home of the British government. Although the name *Big Ben* is used to describe the entire tower, that name actually refers only to the bell that clangs to tell the time. Stories say that Big Ben is named after Sir Benjamin Hall, a large man who oversaw the installation of the bell. And Big Ben is certainly big—the bell weighs more than 13 tons (13,760 kg).

Big Ben's history goes back to 1844, when government officials decided that the Parliament buildings should have a clock tower. The bell was made in 1858 and was first rung a year later. It has been ringing the hours ever since, even when part of the Parliament buildings were bombed during World War II.

The tower is lit up at night, giving people a spectacular view of the massive clock. The minute hands are each 14 feet (4.25 m) long. A special light above the clock face is lit to tell people when Parliament is in session.

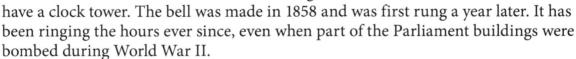

Tourist Attractions

Saint Basil's Cathedral

Saint Basil's Cathedral is the most famous site in Red Square, the center of the city of Moscow. In 1552, the leader of Russia, Czar Ivan the Terrible, decided to build a cathedral to celebrate an important military victory. The cathedral was named after Saint Basil, a saint who was buried on the site. It took just five years, from 1555 to 1560, to build this impressive structure, which looks like no other building in Russia.

The most striking features of Saint Basil's Cathedral are its colorful onion-shaped domes. These domes are painted in a variety of brightly-striped patterns. The inside of the cathedral is also painted brightly with different floral and geometric shapes.

Saint Basil's was not well-liked by the communist government that ruled Russia for most of the 20th century. In fact, Soviet dictator Joseph Stalin threatened to tear it down. But the building survived. It fell into disrepair, however, and was damaged over time by bad weather. Finally, around 2000, the government paid to restore the cathedral. Thousands of visitors come to see Saint Basil's every year. It is one of the most beautiful and well-known sites in Russia.

The Alhambra

The Alhambra is a palace and fortress built on a plateau overlooking Granada, Spain. It was built between 1238 and 1358 by Arab groups from North Africa who ruled Spain at the time. The name *Alhambra* comes from the Arabic words meaning "red one." This name refers to the color of the bricks with which the outer walls are made.

The Alhambra was home to several Spanish rulers. The outside walls of the palace were very plain, but inside were exquisite marble pillars and colorful tile walls and ceilings. There were stunning gardens and fountains everywhere. Because it is always hot in Granada, most of the rooms were open on one side, facing a courtyard.

After falling into disrepair for centuries, the Alhambra was declared a national monument in 1870. The Alhambra is now restored to its original beauty and is one of Spain's most popular tourist attractions.

Tourist Attractions

A. Use the information on the other pages to help you answer the questions.

1. Why did some people not like the Eiffel Tower when it was being built?

   _____

   _____

2. What events could you have seen in the Roman Colosseum?

   _____

   _____

3. What feature of Saint Basil's Cathedral made it a famous site?

   _____

4. What is the Alhambra and where is it located?

   _____

5. What purpose did the Parthenon serve?

   _____

6. What is Big Ben and where is it located?

   _____

   _____

B. Which European tourist attraction would you most like to visit? Explain your answer.

   _____

   _____

   _____

Fine Arts

The people of Europe produce many types of *fine art*, or art that is admired for its beauty rather than its usefulness. Fine arts include painting, sculpture, music, dance, and theater.

Italian Renaissance

The Renaissance was a cultural period occurring roughly between the years 1350 and 1600 AD. It was a time of great artistic expression and creativity in Europe. During this period, Italian artists were especially well-known for their paintings, sculptures, and architecture. Leonardo da Vinci (1452–1519) was one of the most important artists of the Italian Renaissance. He created famous paintings such as the *Mona Lisa* and kept notebooks showing sketches and ideas for inventions that were far ahead of their time, including a helicopter. Michelangelo (1475–1564) was another important Renaissance artist. He created beautiful marble sculptures with religious themes. Between 1508 and 1512, he painted the ceiling of the Sistine Chapel, a church in Vatican City, covering it with detailed scenes from the Bible.

Ballet

Ballet began in France during the late 1500s as a dance performed for the amusement of the king and his court. Later, it developed into a style for dancers who told stories through movement. Over time, ballet spread throughout Europe and became especially popular in Russia, Denmark, Italy, and the UK. Today's professional ballet dancers are highly trained and taught to control their bodies and express themselves through precise steps. Well-known ballet companies such as England's Royal Ballet and Russia's Bolshoi Ballet perform all over the world, entertaining audiences with their grace and beauty.

Theater

Western theater can trace its beginnings back to Greece in the 6th century BC. Throughout ancient Greece, actors presented tales of comedy and tragedy. By the 15th and 16th centuries, theater in Europe had changed into a way to teach religion to uneducated people through dramas called morality plays. During the 1500s, the British playwright William Shakespeare changed theater with his plays about royal history and his outrageous comedies and heart-breaking tragedies.

Modern-day theater in Europe is presented in a variety of forms, from flashy musicals in London's famous West End theater district to dramatic plays that focus on contemporary problems. And Shakespeare's plays are still performed regularly throughout Europe and the world. Despite changes in the theater through the centuries, the themes of happiness, love, jealousy, and greed have stayed the same.

Fine Arts

A. Read each statement. Circle **yes** if it is true or **no** if it is false. Use the information on the other page to help you.

1. The Renaissance occurred between 1350 and 1600.	Yes	No
2. Michelangelo painted the *Mona Lisa*.	Yes	No
3. The Renaissance happened only in Italy.	Yes	No
4. Michelangelo's sculptures featured religious themes.	Yes	No
5. Ballet began in Russia in the 1500s.	Yes	No
6. Ballet dancers once performed to amuse the French court.	Yes	No
7. Ballet became especially popular in Denmark.	Yes	No
8. The Bolshoi Ballet is a well-known Russian ballet company.	Yes	No
9. Theater began in the United Kingdom.	Yes	No
10. Plays during the 15th and 16th centuries taught religious and moral rules.	Yes	No
11. William Shakespeare was a famous sculptor in the 1500s.	Yes	No
12. Modern-day theater includes themes that are very different from when theater first began.	Yes	No

B. Write three things you learned about fine arts in Europe.

1. _____

2. _____

3. _____

Influential Music

From the classical music of past centuries to today's pop and rock, European artists have been making memorable music for hundreds of years.

Classical Music

Beethoven

Classical music began around the 8th century, originating from religious music used in church services. Over the years, the music changed from simple tunes to more elaborate pieces played mainly on the organ, harpsichord, piano, violin, and flute. Johann Sebastian Bach was one of the most famous early classical composers. Bach was born into a musical family in Germany in 1685 and went on to become a church organist and composer. He was known for his complicated orchestra compositions that featured organs, harpsichords, and horns.

Another well-known classical musician was the Austrian composer Wolfgang Amadeus Mozart (1756–1791). Mozart showed great talent at a young age and was playing in the royal courts of Europe by the time he was six years old. Although he lived a short life, Mozart composed over 600 musical works. These include a number of *operas*, which are plays in which the words are sung.

In the late 1700s, another classical composer rose to fame—German-born Ludwig von Beethoven (1770–1827). Beethoven's music featured dramatic and emotional themes. He wrote many works still familiar today, including the *Symphony Number 5, Moonlight Sonata,* and *Für Elise.* The works of Beethoven and other classical composers are regularly performed by orchestras and solo musicians all over the world.

The Beatles

A group of four musicians from Liverpool, England, changed popular music and culture when they burst upon the music scene in 1962. John Lennon, Paul McCartney, George Harrison, and Ringo Starr called themselves The Beatles. They combined American rhythm and blues with lively guitar melodies and cheerful harmonies to create a new kind of "pop" music. The Beatles became wildly popular all over the world. Fans would become so frenzied when The Beatles appeared that their hysteria was named "Beatlemania." Although The Beatles broke up in 1970, their albums continue to sell millions of copies throughout the world. Their songs, including such classics as "Come Together," "Let It Be," and "Yesterday," are still recorded and played by musicians today.

Influential Music

A. Next to each fine art term or name, write the letter of the clue that describes it. Use the information on the other page to help you.

_____ 1. John Lennon

_____ 2. Mozart

_____ 3. Liverpool

_____ 4. classical

_____ 5. rhythm and blues

_____ 6. Bach

_____ 7. "Let It Be"

_____ 8. Beatlemania

_____ 9. *Number 5*

_____ 10. Beethoven

a. a form of music originally played in church

b. an early composer who started out as a church organist

c. an Austrian composer who performed at age 6

d. a symphony written by Beethoven

e. a composer born in Germany in 1770

f. the city that The Beatles were from

g. a member of The Beatles

h. a song by The Beatles

i. a type of American music that influenced The Beatles

j. fan frenzy over a British rock group

B. Use the information on the other page to complete each sentence.

1. Classical music began in the _____ century.

2. Johann Sebastian Bach was born in the country of _____.

3. Mozart composed musical plays called _____.

4. John Lennon, George Harrison, Ringo Starr, and _____ were the four members of The Beatles.

5. Beethoven wrote the _____ *Sonata*.

6. The _____ broke up in 1970.

Popular Sports in Europe

Millions of people in Europe enjoy sports, either as players or spectators. Soccer, which Europeans call football, is by far the most popular sport on the continent. Europe has hundreds of soccer teams, and players such as Portugal's Cristiano Ronaldo and England's David Beckham are international superstars.

Rugby is another popular European sport. This game is similar to soccer, except that players are allowed to run with the ball in their hands and tackle other players, as they do in American football. Rugby is especially popular in the United Kingdom, France, and Italy.

It's not surprising that sports involving ice and snow are enjoyed in the countries of Northern Europe and in Russia. Ice hockey is very popular in both of these areas, as are skiing and snowboarding. These sports are also played in the mountains of Switzerland, France, and Italy. Many Scandinavian athletes enjoy a challenging sport called the biathlon, which combines cross-country skiing with target shooting.

Although basketball was invented in the United States, it has expanded into Europe, especially in the countries of Eastern Europe and the areas around the Mediterranean Sea.

Below is a chart of some of the most popular sports in Europe and where they are played.

Sport	Countries Where Most Popular
Basketball	Slovenia, Serbia, Croatia, Italy, Greece
Bicycle Racing	Belgium, France, Germany, Italy, Netherlands
Cricket	United Kingdom, Netherlands
Ice Hockey	Finland, Sweden, Czech Republic, Austria
Rugby	United Kingdom, France, Ireland, Italy
Soccer	United Kingdom, Italy, Germany, France, Spain
Volleyball	Czech Republic, Slovakia, Italy, Greece

The Olympics

Europe is the birthplace of the Olympics. These games were originally played in ancient Greece thousands of years ago. In 1896, the Games were started again in Athens, Greece. Although the first few modern Olympics were played only in the summer, winter games were soon added. Today, athletes from all over the world gather every two years to compete against each other. Europe has hosted the Olympics many times, including in Berlin, Germany, in 1936; Grenoble, France, in 1968; Moscow, Russia, in 1980; and Turin, Italy, in 2006.

Popular Sports in Europe

A. Circle the correct answer to complete each sentence. Use the information on the other page to help you.

1. The most popular sport in Europe is ____. **soccer** **rugby**

2. In rugby, players are allowed to carry ____. **the ball** **other players**

3. Rugby is especially popular in ____. **France** **Sweden**

4. Ice hockey is popular in ____ Europe. **Southern** **Northern**

5. Cristiano Ronaldo is a Portuguese ____ star. **basketball** **soccer**

6. Basketball is most popular in ____ Europe. **Western** **Eastern**

7. The Scandinavian biathlon combines cross-country skiing with ____. **shooting** **bicycle racing**

8. Volleyball is very popular in ____. **Slovakia** **Finland**

9. Many people in ____ enjoy cricket. **the UK** **Croatia**

10. The first modern Olympic Games were held in ____. **Italy** **Greece**

B. Choose a popular sport in Europe and give three reasons why you would like to play it or watch it.

1. _____

2. _____

3. _____

Major Religions of Europe

The people of Europe practice a number of different religions. While most Europeans are Christian, a large number belong to faiths such as Islam and Judaism. Other religions, such as Hinduism and Sikhism, also have many followers in Europe.

Christianity

There are several Christian *denominations,* or groups, in Europe. About one-third of the population of Europe is Roman Catholic. Catholics follow the guidance of the Pope, who lives in the tiny European country of the Holy See, which is also called Vatican City. More than 80% of the population of Italy, Spain, Portugal, Ireland, Luxembourg, Croatia, and San Marino is Catholic.

The Eastern Orthodox Church also has a large following, particularly in Eastern Europe. This church is similar to the Roman Catholic faith, but followers do not obey the Pope's authority. Russia, Albania, Bulgaria, Greece, and Romania all have large populations of Eastern Orthodox followers.

During the 1600s, a new form of Christianity called Protestantism arose in Germany and other parts of Europe. Protestants had major disagreements with Roman Catholics and decided to split from the church during this period. Today, more than 80% of the people in Denmark, Sweden, Norway, and Finland are Protestant.

Islam

Islam first came to Europe during the 7th century, when Muslim rulers from Africa conquered parts of the Iberian Peninsula. Later, Islam spread to Russia, Albania, Macedonia, and other parts of southeastern Europe. In recent years, large numbers of Muslims, or people who practice Islam, have moved to the United Kingdom, France, the Netherlands, Switzerland, Germany, and Austria.

Judaism

Jewish people once made up a large part of the population of Germany, Russia, and Poland, but violence against them in the early 20th century and during the Holocaust (1941–1945) dramatically reduced their population. Large numbers of Jews also once lived in Spain, but they were driven out in the 15th century. Today, France has the largest population of Jews in Europe, followed by the UK, Germany, Russia, and Italy.

Other Religions

Hinduism spread through Europe as people immigrated to the continent from India, Pakistan, and other Asian countries. Currently, there are more than 1.5 million Hindus living throughout Europe. Sikhism is another faith that comes from India. The greatest number of Sikhs live in the United Kingdom but account for just over 1% of the country's population.

Major Religions of Europe

A. Read each statement. Circle **yes** if it is true or **no** if it is false. Use the information on the other page to help you.

1. Over half of all Europeans are Roman Catholic.   **Yes**   **No**

2. Islam first came to Europe from Africa.   **Yes**   **No**

3. During the Holocaust, the number of Jews in Europe   **Yes**   **No**
   fell dramatically.

4. Sikhism and Hinduism came to Europe from countries in   **Yes**   **No**
   North America.

5. Protestants and Eastern Orthodox Church members follow   **Yes**   **No**
   the guidance of the Pope.

6. The Eastern Orthodox Church is similar to the Roman   **Yes**   **No**
   Catholic Church.

7. Large numbers of Protestants live in Northern Europe.   **Yes**   **No**

8. The number of Muslims in Europe is decreasing.   **Yes**   **No**

B. List the seven religions of Europe discussed on the other page.

1. _____

2. _____

3. _____

4. _____

5. _____

6. _____

7. _____

European Cuisine

Many foods from Europe have become popular elsewhere in the world. Here are just a few European dishes that are enjoyed in the United States and other countries.

Food	Ingredients	Country of Origin
Belgian waffles	puffy, flat cakes topped with powdered sugar, cream, or fruit	Belgium
borscht	cold or hot soup made with beets	Russia
bratwurst	thick, juicy sausage served on warm, crusty rolls	Germany
Cornish pasty	meat and vegetables baked inside a thick folded crust, eaten with the hands	United Kingdom
goulash	stew made with beef, onions, other vegetables, and a spice called *paprika*	Hungary
paella (pie-AY-uh)	rice mixed with vegetables, meat, seafood, and a spice called *saffron*, cooked in a large pan	Spain
pierogi (pih-ROH-gy)	dumplings filled with potatoes, cheese, and onions	Poland
pizza	flat bread topped with tomato sauce, cheese, meat, or vegetables	Italy

Fun Food Facts

- In 1889, a chef in Naples, Italy, was asked to create a special pie to honor the visiting Queen Margherita. He created a pizza topped with red tomatoes, white cheese, and green basil to recreate the colors of the Italian flag. This type of pizza is still called a margherita pizza today.

- The word *bratwurst* comes from the old German word *brät,* meaning "finely chopped meat," and *wurst,* meaning "sausage."

- English miners often brought Cornish pasties into the mines to eat. The baker would carve each man's initials into the crust to let out steam and make it easy for each man to find his lunch.

European Cuisine

A. Write the letter of the country of origin that matches each type of European cuisine. Use the information on the other page to help you.

_____ 1. Belgian waffles   a. Hungary

_____ 2. borscht   b. Italy

_____ 3. goulash   c. Russia

_____ 4. Cornish pasty   d. Spain

_____ 5. paella   e. Poland

_____ 6. bratwurst   f. United Kingdom

_____ 7. pierogi   g. Belgium

_____ 8. pizza   h. Germany

B. Answer the questions.

1. Have you eaten any of the European foods listed on the other page? If so, which ones?

_____

_____

2. If you answered "yes" to number 1, which food was your favorite and why?

_____

_____

3. Which European food that you have *not* eaten would you most like to try? Why?

_____

_____

Celebrations

Europe's many different countries and cultures hold a wide range of special celebrations. Here are two colorful and exciting celebrations that take place in Europe.

The Running of the Bulls

The Running of the Bulls has been a tradition in Pamplona, Spain, for hundreds of years. The holiday started as a religious festival during the 13th century. Later, the religious celebration was combined with a bullfighting fiesta, music, dancing, and a market day.

A traditional part of the festival was to release a herd of bulls at 8:00 every morning from July 7 to July 14. The bulls ran through the narrow streets, with people trying to run ahead of the stampeding herd. The race ended at the bullring, where bullfights were held later in the afternoon. Few people outside of Pamplona knew about the Running of the Bulls until 1926, when popular American author Ernest Hemingway wrote about the event in a novel. Today, thousands of people flock to Pamplona every July to witness or take part in this exciting, but dangerous, spectacle.

Oktoberfest

Oktoberfest is an annual event held in Germany. Despite its name, this event actually begins on the third weekend in September and ends on the first Sunday in October. Oktoberfest began as a celebration of the royal wedding of Crown Prince Ludwig to Princess Therese on October 12, 1810. The citizens of the city of Munich were invited to join the festivities, which included horse races and other events. The celebration was repeated every year, and new events were added, including a carnival, a parade where people wore traditional costumes, and a concert featuring brass bands. Over the years, stands selling beer and food were added, and these refreshments have become a big part of the festival. Today, Munich's Oktoberfest calls itself the largest festival in the world, with thousands of people from around the world coming to join the fun.

Celebrations

A. Unscramble each word to finish the sentence.

1. The Running of the Bulls is held in _____ every year.
   lomanpap

2. The Running of the Bulls started as a _____ festival.
   lgosiurei

3. During the festival, people run through the streets, trying to stay ahead of

   _____ bulls.
   gasmepdint

4. Ernest Hemingway, a popular _____ author, wrote about the Running of the Bulls.
   camerina

5. Oktoberfest is held in _____.
   gamyren

6. The festival actually starts in _____.
   tesmeperb

7. Originally, Oktoberfest celebrated a _____ wedding.
   yalor

8. Many people wear traditional _____ during Oktoberfest.
   tescmuos

9. The city of _____ holds a large Oktoberfest.
   cinumh

B. Which festival would you like to attend? Explain your answer.

_____

_____

_____

Review

Use words from the box to complete the crossword puzzle.

Beatles

borscht

Christian

Colosseum

Eiffel

football

Michelangelo

Pamplona

Across

4. Ancient Romans went to the _____ to see events and contests.

6. _____, or soccer, is the most popular sport in Europe.

8. Most people in Europe belong to a _____ religion.

Down

1. _____ is a popular Russian soup.

2. The Running of the Bulls is held in _____, Spain.

3. _____ painted the ceiling of the Sistine Chapel.

5. The _____ were a British band who changed popular culture.

7. The _____ Tower was once the tallest structure in the world.

The 7 Continents: Europe • EMC 3735 • © Evan-Moor Corp.

Assessment

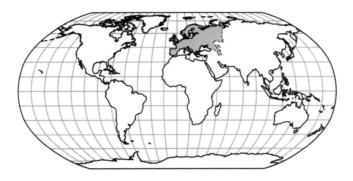

This section provides two cumulative assessments that you can use to evaluate students' acquisition of the information presented in this book. The first assessment requires students to identify selected cities, countries, landforms, and bodies of water on a combined physical and political map. The second assessment is a two-page multiple-choice test covering information from all sections of the book. Use one or both assessments as culminating activities for your class's study of Europe.

CONTENTS

Name _____

Map Test

Write the name of the country, capital city, landform, or body of water that matches each number. Use the words in the box to help you.

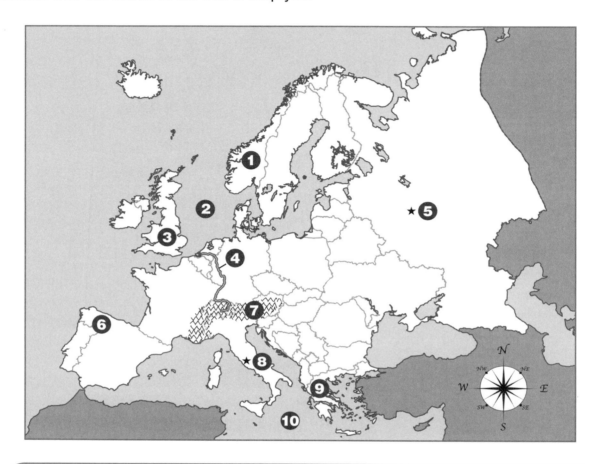

Mediterranean Sea	Greece	The Alps	Moscow	United Kingdom
Iberian Peninsula	Rome	North Sea	Norway	Rhine River

1. _____   6. _____

2. _____   7. _____

3. _____   8. _____

4. _____   9. _____

5. _____   10. _____

Multiple-Choice Test

Fill in the bubble to answer each question or complete each sentence.

1. Europe is the sixth-largest continent in the world in ____.

   Ⓐ size

   Ⓑ population

   Ⓒ both size and population

   Ⓓ number of cities and countries

2. Which continent shares a land border with Europe?

   Ⓐ Africa

   Ⓑ Asia

   Ⓒ North America

   Ⓓ South America

3. In which two hemispheres is Europe mostly located?

   Ⓐ Northern and Southern

   Ⓑ Eastern and Western

   Ⓒ Southern and Western

   Ⓓ Northern and Eastern

4. Europe is divided into ____ regions.

   Ⓐ four

   Ⓑ six

   Ⓒ eight

   Ⓓ ten

5. Which country in Europe has the largest population?

   Ⓐ Germany

   Ⓑ Denmark

   Ⓒ United Kingdom

   Ⓓ Russia

6. Which two countries are islands?

   Ⓐ Spain and Italy

   Ⓑ Iceland and Malta

   Ⓒ Iceland and Denmark

   Ⓓ Italy and Malta

7. Which mountain range separates Europe and Asia?

   Ⓐ The Alps

   Ⓑ Carpathian Mountains

   Ⓒ Pyrenees Mountains

   Ⓓ Ural Mountains

8. Russia's ____ River empties into the Caspian Sea.

   Ⓐ Volga

   Ⓑ Thames

   Ⓒ Rhine

   Ⓓ Seine

Multiple-Choice Test

9. Which body of water is *not* found in Europe?

Ⓐ Mediterranean Sea

Ⓑ Adriatic Sea

Ⓒ Baltic Sea

Ⓓ Caribbean Sea

10. Two countries that produce oil from the North Sea are _____.

Ⓐ Norway and Italy

Ⓑ Greece and the Netherlands

Ⓒ Denmark and Norway

Ⓓ United Kingdom and Iceland

11. Which country is Europe's top producer of olive oil?

Ⓐ Spain

Ⓑ Italy

Ⓒ France

Ⓓ Germany

12. Which of these animals is found in Northern Europe's boreal forests?

Ⓐ bison

Ⓑ tiger

Ⓒ alligator

Ⓓ elk

13. Why are cattle, pigs, and sheep called *livestock*?

Ⓐ They are wild animals.

Ⓑ They are raised by people as a resource.

Ⓒ They are all endangered species.

Ⓓ They live in state parks.

14. Which religion was founded in Germany?

Ⓐ Islam

Ⓑ Protestantism

Ⓒ Roman Catholicism

Ⓓ Judaism

15. _____ is the largest crop grown in Europe.

Ⓐ wheat

Ⓑ oats

Ⓒ corn

Ⓓ potatoes

16. A major tourist attraction in Spain is _____.

Ⓐ the Parthenon

Ⓑ the Colosseum

Ⓒ Big Ben

Ⓓ the Alhambra

Note Takers

This section provides four note-taker forms that give students the opportunity to culminate their study of Europe by doing independent research on places or animals of their choice. (Some suggested topics are given below.) Students may use printed reference materials or Internet sites to gather information on their topics. A cover page is also provided so that students may create a booklet of note takers and any other reproducible pages from the book that you would like students to save.

FORMS

Select a physical feature of Europe. Write notes about it to complete each section.

_____
(Name of Physical Feature)

N
W E
S

Location

_____
_____
_____

Interesting Facts

_____
_____
_____
_____
_____
_____
_____
_____
_____
_____
_____
_____

Description

_____
_____
_____
_____
_____
_____
_____
_____
_____
_____
_____
_____

Animals or Plants

_____
_____
_____
_____

Name _____

Draw a European animal. Write notes about it to complete each section.

_____
(Name of Animal)

Habitat

_____
_____
_____
_____

Endangered? (Yes) (No)

Physical Characteristics

_____
_____
_____
_____

Diet

_____
_____
_____
_____

Behaviors

_____
_____
_____
_____

Enemies/Defenses

_____
_____
_____
_____

Draw a European tourist attraction. Then write notes about it to complete each section.

_____

(Name of Tourist Attraction)

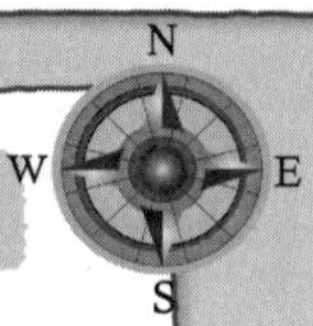

N

W   E

S

Location

_____
_____
_____
_____

Description

_____
_____
_____
_____
_____
_____
_____
_____
_____
_____
_____
_____

Interesting Facts

_____
_____
_____
_____

Name _____

Select a European city you would like to visit. Write notes about it to complete each section.

My Trip to _____
(Name of City)

Location

_____

_____

_____

_____

How I Would Get There

_____

_____

_____

_____

Things I Would See and Do

_____

_____

_____

_____

_____

_____

_____

_____

_____

Foods I Would Eat

_____

_____

_____

_____

Learning the Language

How to Say "Hello"

_____

How to Say "Goodbye"

_____

EUROPE

Page 5

1. B 2. A 3. B 4. C 5. B

Page 6

A. Asia, south, North America, Arctic, south, Atlantic

B. Students should color Africa green, color North America yellow, and use blue to circle the Atlantic Ocean. They should also draw a panda on Asia.

Page 9

A. 1. c   4. e   7. g
   2. f   5. d   8. i
   3. h   6. b   9. a

B.

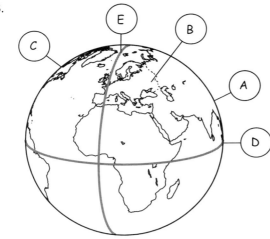

Page 11

A. 1. equator   6. latitude lines
   2. prime meridian 7. 15 degrees
   3. north   8. parallels
   4. 15°E   9. 45°N
   5. 90°N   10. meridians

B. Because southern Italy is located north of the equator and east of the prime meridian, the latitude and longitude lines of its absolute location are labeled in degrees north and east.

Page 12

A. 1. Yes   4. No   7. Yes
   2. No   5. Yes   8. Yes
   3. No   6. No   9. Yes

B. Three—Europe, Africa, and Antarctica

Page 14

Across   **Down**
3. Northern   1. projection
4. Europe   2. longitude
5. Atlantic   6. absolute
7. equator
8. hemispheres

Page 17

1. C   2. B   3. C   4. A   5. B

Page 18

A. Students should color each bar a different color.

Page 19

B. 1. tripled   5. 700
   2. 2050   6. 702
   3. slow   7. decline
   4. 547   8. 1950–1970

C. Answers will vary—e.g.,
   1. In which year was the population of Europe the highest? Answer: 2010.
   2. About how many people lived in Europe in 1970? Answer: 660 million.

Page 21

Students should color the nine countries of Western Europe green, the 10 countries of Eastern Europe orange, the 16 countries of Southern Europe red, and the 10 countries of Northern Europe green.

Page 22

A. Answers will vary—e.g.,
   1. The European part of Russia has over 1 million square miles more than Ukraine.
   2. Sweden is the fifth-largest country in Europe.
   3. France is 42,280 square kilometers bigger than Spain.

Page 23

B. Students should color Russia, Ukraine, France, Spain, and Sweden different colors and then complete the map key.

The Five Largest Countries
1. European part of Russia   Colors will vary.
2. Ukraine   Colors will vary.
3. France   Colors will vary.
4. Spain   Colors will vary.
5. Sweden   Colors will vary.

Page 24

A. 1. d   6. a
   2. c   7. b
   3. j   8. e
   4. f   9. g
   5. h   10. i

B. 1. four
   2. five

Page 25

C. Answers will vary—e.g.,
   1. Germany has the second-highest population in Europe, with more than 82 million people.
   2. Romania has a population of 22,181,287.
   3. The European part of Russia is more populated than any other country in Europe.

Page 26

A. 1. No   6. Yes
   2. No   7. Yes
   3. Yes   8. Yes
   4. Yes   9. No
   5. No   10. Yes

B. Students should color the nine countries of Western Europe a different color. Then they should complete the caption. Captions will vary—e.g., Western Europe includes both large countries such as Germany and France, and small ones such as Monaco and Liechtenstein.

Page 28

A. 1. 260 million   5. Slovakia
   2. Russia   6. Russia
   3. large populations   7. Prague
   4. four   8. Hungary

Page 29

B. Students should color Russia, Poland, Romania, Ukraine, and the Czech Republic red.

Page 30

A. Students should color Italy, Greece, Spain, Portugal, and Serbia a different color. Then they should complete the map key.

Page 31

The Five Largest Countries	Color
1. Spain	Colors will vary.
2. Italy	Colors will vary.
3. Greece	Colors will vary.
4. Portugal	Colors will vary.
5. Serbia	Colors will vary.

B. Captions will vary—e.g., Spain has the largest area of any country in Western Europe, while the Holy See has the smallest.

Page 32

A. 1. No   6. Yes
   2. Yes   7. Yes
   3. Yes   8. No
   4. No   9. Yes
   5. Yes   10. No

B. Students should color Iceland, Norway, Sweden, Denmark, and Finland orange; the United Kingdom and Ireland green; and Estonia, Latvia, and Lithuania red. Captions will vary—e.g., The 10 countries of Northern Europe can be divided into three regions—Scandinavia, the British Isles, and the Baltic states.

Page 35

A.

B. 1. d   6. b
   2. h   7. e
   3. a   8. j
   4. f   9. c
   5. i   10. g

Page 36

1. communist
2. republics
3. Czechoslovakia
4. democracy
5. seven

Page 38

A. 1. Yes 6. Yes
2. Yes 7. No
3. No 8. Yes
4. No 9. No
5. No 10. No

B. Students should color the 27 EU countries green.

Page 40

Across
1. Russia
6. communist
7. Paris
8. Union
9. ten

Down
2. Sweden
3. Germany
4. Eastern
5. Holy See

Page 43

1. A   2. A   3. D   4. C   5. B

Page 44

A. 1. the Alps 5. North European Plain
2. Mount Elbrus 6. Iberian Peninsula
3. British Isles 7. Italian Peninsula
4. Ural Mountains 8. Scandinavian Peninsula

B. Answers will vary—e.g.,
1. Europe has an extremely jagged coastline.
2. Forests cover nearly half the continent of Europe.

Page 47

A. 1. Yes 6. Yes
2. Yes 7. Yes
3. No 8. No
4. No 9. Yes
5. No 10. No

B. 1. Scandinavian
2. Iberian
3. Balkan
4. Scandinavian
5. Italian
6. Jutland

Page 49

A. Students should circle the following islands in the following colors:
Green: Guernsey, Ireland, Isle of Man, Jersey, United Kingdom
Yellow: Crete, Greek Isles
Purple: Corsica
Orange: Faroe Islands
Blue: Iceland
Brown: Malta
Red: Sardinia, Sicily

B.

```
U Q N E T U Y C R E T E M F V
S C J S A L T I C E L A N D K
A B L C N R M O U D K B M E L
R V F O R T I A N L A R B L A
D I I R G R A C L S E J A I R
I R S S K I C H T S P O B R E
N N L I W I T Y K A H L E L
I J A C M A C F A R O E R N A
A I F A R Y L I F L W T B L N
G R M Y W U F D L R Q D A D
D D G U E R N S E Y E U M D P
O U N I T E D K I N G D O M P
```

Page 51

1. Mount Elbrus 6. Etna
2. Caucasus 7. Iberian
3. Gerlachovsky Peak 8. Ural
4. tallest 9. Musala
5. Alps 10. Mount Mulhacen

Page 53

Italy, Vesuvius, 10,000, Naples, erupt, Etna, million, 2010, Stromboli, 2,000, lava, Iceland, Hekla, 4,892, 2000, ash, planes

Page 55

A. 1. c 6. e
2. j 7. f
3. h 8. a
4. b 9. d
5. i 10. g

B. 1. boreal 5. Mediterranean
2. temperate 6. boreal
3. Mediterranean 7. mountain
4. mountain

Page 57

A. 1. permafrost
2. summer
3. a cold area where soil is frozen between 10 and 35 inches deep
4. Russia, Finland, Iceland, Norway, and Sweden
5. Answers will vary—e.g., reindeer, lemmings, snowy owls
6. a soggy land covered in marshes, bogs, lakes, and streams

B. 1. Yes 5. No
2. No 6. Yes
3. No 7. No
4. Yes

Page 58

A.

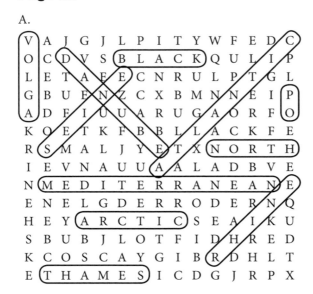

Page 59

B. Students should use blue to circle the Arctic and Atlantic oceans, the Black, Mediterranean, and North seas, and the Danube, Po, Rhine, Seine, Thames, and Volga rivers. They should use red to circle the remaining bodies of water on the map. Then they should complete the caption. Answers will vary—e.g., Europe is bordered by two oceans and several major seas.

Page 61

1. North
2. Mediterranean
3. Norwegian
4. Adriatic
5. salty
6. Baltic
7. Black
8. Atlantic
9. Africa
10. Japan
11. Caspian

Page 63

A. 1. g   6. a
   2. f   7. i
   3. h   8. c
   4. b   9. e
   5. d

B. 1. No   5. Yes
   2. Yes   6. Yes
   3. No   7. Yes
   4. Yes   8. No

Page 65

A. 1. fjords   6. halfway
   2. Sognefjord   7. three
   3. Norway   8. Hardangerfjord
   4. 10,000   9. glaciers
   5. waterfalls   10. Sognefjord

B. Answers will vary—e.g.,
   1. The fjords are filled with salt water from the sea.
   2. Large cruise ships sail into Geirangerfjord.
   3. Hardangerfjord is south of both Sognefjord and Geirangerfjord.

Page 66

Across	Down
3. fjords	1. volcanoes
5. Rhine	2. Mediterranean
6. tundra	4. conifers
7. Balkan	

Page 69

1. B   2. A   3. C   4. C   5. B

Page 71

A. 1. No   6. Yes
   2. Yes   7. No
   3. No   8. No
   4. Yes   9. No
   5. Yes   10. Yes

B. 1. 98,700,000 gallons
   2. 373,650,000 liters
   3. a gallon is about four times larger than a liter

Page 73

A. commercial, tons, Russia, Iceland, tuna, salmon, Norway

B. Answers will vary—e.g.,
   1. Fish such as cod, tuna, salmon, and haddock are caught in the Atlantic Ocean, North Sea, and Mediterranean Sea.
   2. In Europe, some fish are raised in farms instead of caught in the wild.
   3. There are nearly 800,000 people in Europe who are involved in the fishing industry.

Page 75

A. 1. h   6. g
   2. e   7. b
   3. f   8. j
   4. a   9. c
   5. i   10. d

B. 1. wheat   4. Corn
   2. exported   5. oats
   3. calories   6. Oatmeal

Page 77

A. 1. thousands
   2. the world
   3. skin products
   4. feet
   5. green
   6. Greece
   7. leaves
   8. Greece
   9. Spain
   10. Italy

B. Answers will vary—e.g., Olives are grown on the coast of the Mediterranean Sea in countries such as Spain, Italy, Greece, and Portugal.

Page 78

Students should color Italy green, France red, Spain yellow, Germany orange, and Portugal brown.

Page 79

A. 1. Italy
   2. Spain, France, and Italy
   3. because the vines thrive in the rocky soil where other crops cannot grow
   4. Grapes are first harvested from the vines between August and October. Then the grapes are pressed for their juices. Yeast is added to the juice to ferment it. Finally, the wine is put in a bottle and stored for at least one year.

B.

Rank	Country	Color
1	Italy	green
2	France	red
3	Spain	yellow
4	Germany	orange
5	Portugal	brown

Page 81

A. 1. No
   2. No
   3. Yes
   4. No
   5. Yes
   6. Yes
   7. No
   8. No
   9. Yes
   10. No

B. Answers will vary—e.g.,
   1. Pigs are a valuable food source for Europeans because they provide meat to make pork chops, bacon, loin, and sausage.
   2. Sheep provide Europeans with meat, cheese, and wool.
   3. Europeans raise cattle for meat, farm labor, and dairy products, including milk and cheese.

Page 83

A. 1. Timber is wood that can be used for building and to make paper products.
   2. They provide people with timber. They are a home for wild animals and plants. Their trees produce oxygen.
   3. chopping down trees to clear land and acid rain
   4. They can reduce pollution, stop cutting down so many trees, and create more national parks.

B. Answers will vary—e.g.,

Tree	Use
beech	furniture
elm	docks and piers
larch	fences
willow	toys

Page 87

A. 1. Iberian lynx
   2. red fox
   3. Barbary macaque
   4. badger
   5. Hermann's tortoise
   6. red fox
   7. osprey
   8. Iberian lynx
   9. osprey
   10. Barbary macaque
   11. Hermann's tortoise
   12. badger

B. Answers will vary—e.g., I would like to learn more about the Barbary macaque because I think it's interesting that it's the only monkey in all of Europe.

Page 88

Across	Down
5. badgers	1. wheat
7. livestock	2. vineyards
	3. fossil
	4. aquaculture
	6. olive
	8. timber

Page 91

1. B   2. C   3. A   4. A   5. D

Page 95

A. 1. because they thought it was useless and believed it might cause problems for birds flying overhead
   2. contests where men tried to kill wild animals, gladiator fights, and mock sea battles
   3. its colorful onion-shaped domes
   4. a fortress and a palace located in Granada, Spain
   5. It was a temple dedicated to the goddess Athena.
   6. a bell that rings the time in the clock tower above the Houses of Parliament in London

B. Answers will vary—e.g., I'm most interested in visiting the Colosseum because I think it would be interesting to see such an ancient place where many games and battles took place.

Page 97

A. 1. Yes   7. Yes
   2. No   8. Yes
   3. No   9. No
   4. Yes   10. Yes
   5. No   11. No
   6. Yes   12. No

B. Answers will vary—e.g.,
   1. Ballet dancers tell stories through movement.
   2. Ancient Greek actors performed comedic and tragic plays.
   3. Leonardo da Vinci kept a notebook full of ideas for inventions.

Page 99

A. 1. g   6. b
   2. c   7. h
   3. f   8. j
   4. a   9. d
   5. i   10. e

B. 1. 8th
   2. Germany
   3. operas
   4. Paul McCartney
   5. *Moonlight*
   6. Beatles

Page 101

A. 1. soccer   6. Eastern
   2. the ball   7. shooting
   3. France   8. Slovakia
   4. Northern   9. the UK
   5. soccer   10. Greece

B. Answers will vary—e.g.,
   1. I would like to play soccer because I like to kick.
   2. I would like to watch soccer because the game is exciting.
   3. I would like to watch soccer because I am a fan of Cristiano Ronaldo.

Page 103

A. 1. No   5. No
   2. Yes   6. Yes
   3. Yes   7. Yes
   4. No   8. No

B. 1. Roman Catholicism
   2. Eastern Orthodox
   3. Protestantism
   4. Islam
   5. Judaism
   6. Hinduism
   7. Sikhism

Page 105

A. 1. g   5. d
   2. c   6. h
   3. a   7. e
   4. f   8. b

B. Answers will vary—e.g.,
   1. Yes, Belgian waffles, bratwurst, paella, pierogi, and pizza
   2. Pizza is my favorite because I love the melty cheese and the crunchy crust.
   3. I would like to try a Cornish pasty because it sounds like fun to eat with your hands.

Page 107

A. 1. Pamplona   6. September
   2. religious   7. royal
   3. stampeding   8. costumes
   4. American   9. Munich
   5. Germany

B. Answers will vary—e.g.,
I would like to go to Oktoberfest to see the costumes, try the food, and watch the parade.

Page 108

Across	Down
4. Colosseum	1. Borscht
6. Football	2. Pamplona
8. Christian	3. Michelangelo
	5. Beatles
	7. Eiffel

Page 110

1. Norway   6. Iberian Peninsula
2. North Sea   7. The Alps
3. United Kingdom   8. Rome
4. Rhine River   9. Greece
5. Moscow   10. Mediterranean Sea

Page 111

1. A   2. B   3. D   4. A   5. D   6. B   7. D   8. A

Page 112

9. D   10. C   11. A   12. D   13. B   14. B
15. A   16. D

Daily Geography

Skill: Cooperative Solutions
Essential Element 4: Standard 13

ANSWER KEY

Note: Not all questions can be answered with information from the map. Students will have to use their mental map skills to locate places on the map.

Monday
1. 6; Hawaiian-Aleutian, Alaskan, Pacific, Mountain, Central, and Eastern Times
2. one hour

Tuesday
1. earlier
2. Eastern Time

Wednesday
1. Hawaiian-Aleutian Time
2. 11:00 A.M.

Thursday
1. 10:00 P.M.
2. North Dakota, South Dakota, Nebraska, Kansas, and Texas

Friday
1. No, it's 2:00 A.M. and Grandfather is probably sleeping.
2. It is Daylight Saving Time.

Challenge
Answers will vary, but students should make up two questions and provide answers to the questions.

Time Zones of the United States

Introducing the Map

Ask students what it would be like if every community in the United States used a different time. The obvious answer is that people would be confused and many problems would be created. To avoid this confusion, a cooperative system was designed called *standard time zones*. Talk about the advantages of having regional time zones.

Explain the concept of time zones. A day is 24 hours long—the time it takes Earth to complete one rotation on its axis. Earth is divided into 24 time zones. The United States is divided into six of those twenty-four time zones.

Show students the Time Zones of the United States map. Tell students that each zone uses a time one hour different from its neighboring zones. The hours are earlier to the west of each zone and later to the east.

Go over all the names of the time zones and have students notice the one hour difference between each of them. Talk about how Alaska is so large that it covers two time zones. Explain that some of the Aleutian Islands of Alaska are so far west that scientists placed them with Hawaii, thus creating Hawaiian-Aleutian Time.

Ask students which time zone Chicago, Illinois, is in. They will probably say Central Time. Then ask them: If it is 3:00 P.M. in Chicago, what time is it in Denver? The answer is 2:00 P.M. Ask students a couple more questions, each time changing the local times to help students understand the concept.

Extend the lesson to discuss daylight saving time. This is a plan in which clocks are set one hour ahead of standard time for a certain period of time. The plan provides for an additional hour of daylight. It begins on the first Sunday in April and ends on the last Sunday in October. Most states choose to go on daylight saving time, but several don't. Talk about how that complicates things.

Introducing Vocabulary

daylight saving time a plan in which clocks are set one hour ahead of standard time for a specific period of time

standard time zone a region in which the same time is used

time zone a region in which the same time is used; Earth is divided into 24 time zones

Time Zones of the United States

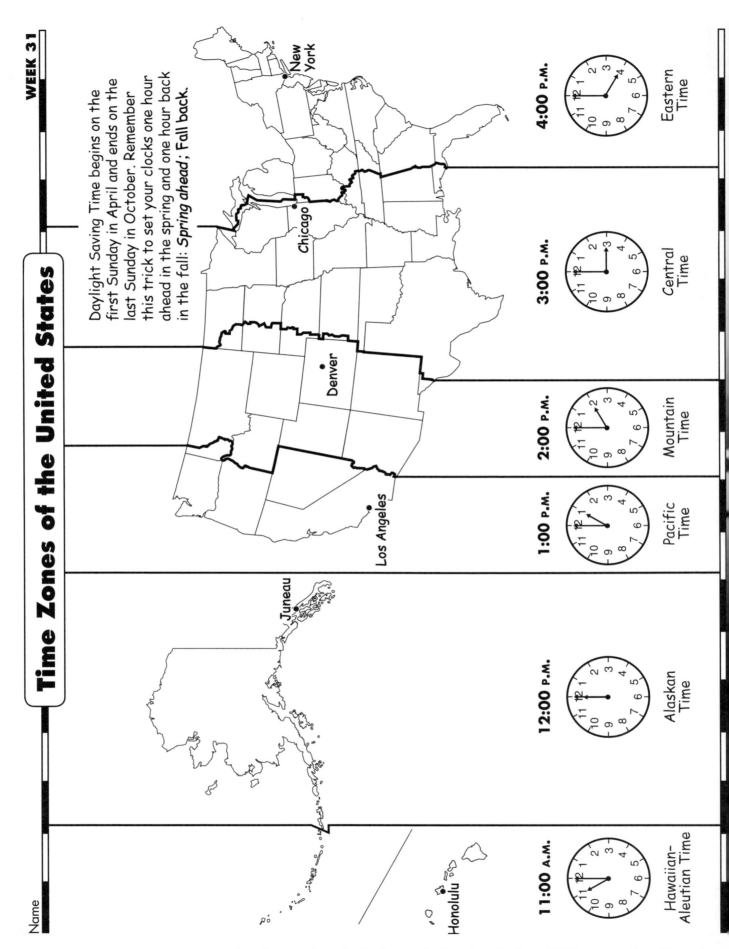

Daylight Saving Time begins on the first Sunday in April and ends on the last Sunday in October. Remember this trick to set your clocks one hour ahead in the spring and one hour back in the fall: *Spring ahead; Fall back.*

New York

Chicago

Denver

Los Angeles

Juneau

Honolulu

4:00 P.M.
Eastern Time

3:00 P.M.
Central Time

2:00 P.M.
Mountain Time

1:00 P.M.
Pacific Time

12:00 P.M.
Alaskan Time

11:00 A.M.
Hawaiian–Aleutian Time

Time Zones of the United States

Monday

1. The United States is divided into how many standard time zones? Name them from west to east.

   _____

   _____

   _____

2. What is the time difference between each neighboring time zone?

   _____

Tuesday

1. Are the hours earlier or later to the west of each time zone?

   _____

2. Cities in the Northeast region are part of which time zone?

   _____

Wednesday

1. Which time zone includes Hawaii and some of the western islands of Alaska?

   _____

2. If it is 1:00 P.M. in Chicago, what time is it in Los Angeles?

   _____

Name _____

Time Zones of the United States

Thursday

1. If it is midnight in Chicago, what time is it in Seattle, Washington?

    _____

2. Which states have areas that are part of Central and Mountain Time Zones?

    _____

    _____

    _____

Friday

1. If you live in Honolulu and it is 9:00 P.M., is it a good time to call your grandfather in New York? Why or why not?

    _____

    _____

2. It is the first Sunday in April and clocks have been set one hour ahead. Why?

    _____

Challenge

Make up two time zone questions. Write your questions on the back of the map. Don't forget to include the answer. Pair up with a classmate and ask each other the time zone questions.